The Older Worker

The Older Worker

Effective Strategies
for Management and
Human Resource
Development

Noreen Hale

Jossey-Bass Publishers
San Francisco • Oxford • 1990

THE OLDER WORKER
Effective Strategies for Management and Human Resource Development
by Noreen Hale

Copyright © 1990 by: Jossey-Bass Inc., Publishers
350 Sansome Street
San Francisco, California 94104
&
Jossey-Bass Limited
Headington Hill Hall
Oxford OX3 0BW

Library of Congress Cataloging-in-Publication Data

Hale, Noreen, date.
    The older worker : effective strategies for management and human
resource development / Noreen Hale. — 1st ed.
        p.   cm. — (The Jossey-Bass management series)
    Includes bibliographical references and index.
    ISBN 1-55542-284-5 (alk. paper)
    1. Aged — Employment — United States.   2. Age and employment —
United States.   3. Occupational retraining — United States.   I. Title.
II. Series.
HD6280.H35   1990
658.3'042 — dc20   90-4583
                                                                                    CIP

Manufactured in the United States of America

The paper in this book meets the guidelines for
permanence and durability of the Committee on
Production Guidelines for Book Longevity of
the Council on Library Resources.

JACKET DESIGN BY WILLI BAUM

FIRST EDITION

Code 9082

The Jossey-Bass Management Series

Consulting Editors
Human Resources

Leonard Nadler
Zeace Nadler
College Park, Maryland

Contents

Preface

Changing demographics portend a work force with fewer sixteen- to twenty-four-year-olds, and a female-dominated, multicultural, and multigenerational labor pool. Consequently, managers face the challenge of cultivating skills in managing a different work-force profile. *The Older Worker* offers strategies for effectively managing older workers, and for designing and conducting learning programs for and about them. It includes numerous concrete suggestions for programs on human resources (HR) and human resource development (HRD) related to workers aged fifty and over in such areas as management training, action planning, and meeting the unique needs of older female workers in the 1990s.

The purpose of this book is twofold: First, it endeavors to assemble what is currently known about older workers, including HR and HRD programs for and about them. Taken together, the programs described here make up a portrait of how older workers are being utilized. From this information, readers can select appropriate ideas and customize them to fit their own organizations. Second, the work illuminates the characteristics, needs, and life changes of older workers. It is hoped that such discussion of the mature employee as a person experiencing growth and development will encourage creative, relevant, and appropriate programming.

In this book, *older worker* refers to employees fifty years of age or more. While I have emphasized the efforts being made to bring retirees back into the organization, I have also treated endeavors to buck the trend toward early retirement of qualified and valuable personnel. *The Older Worker* describes numerous management practices from the corporate sector that are also applicable to the public and not-for-profit arenas. An educational, charitable, or health care organization can imaginatively modify, to suit its own needs, older-worker programs developed by an electronics firm. The book considers matters concerning older workers that are of interest to senior management as policymakers, to department and division managers as supervisors of older employees, to HR professionals as interpreters and architects of personnel policies and practices, and to HRD professionals as designers, managers, and implementers of learning programs for and about older workers.

Current works on this topic narrowly consider the older individual either from a gerontological or from a management and human resources viewpoint. *The Older Worker* integrates the perspective of the psychosocial facets of aging with that of managing and formulating career development and learning programs for the older worker. It creates an interface between gerontology and management's responsibility for human resource development by synthesizing the available data on corporate programs for and about older workers, and then organizing it in a humanistic, life-development perspective.

Finally, *The Older Worker* provides general guidelines for managers of and program designers for older workers. It does not purport to be encyclopedic in its treatment. However, specialized topics such as age discrimination, while not treated in depth in the text, are handled through the Resources for Further Information section found toward the end of the book.

Audience

Consistent with the dual purpose of this book, I offer a holistic base of knowledge and practice about older-worker concerns to audiences in five categories. The first audience is that of general managers, especially HR managers in organizations that employ or are considering employing older persons. Grounded in an understanding of changing demographics, they will be in a better position to understand, lead, and inform personnel accurately about older-worker issues. The book includes a chapter on managing older workers that addresses key points to consider and put into practice.

A second audience is that of HRD managers. *The Older Worker* provides this group with an opportunity to grasp both the suitable management skills and the learning theory, content, and process they will need for supervising and overseeing the development of learning programs for and about older employees. For example, the book offers ideas on what younger supervisors need to know in order to both anticipate and offset decline in general satisfaction among their older subordinates.

HRD practitioners who are not managers make up a third audience for the book. By applying information provided throughout the book, they will be better able to orient their training, education, and development programs to the needs and values of the older workers in their firms. They will also be in a better position to offer appropriate programs for and about older employees to all levels of the company. Moreover, *The Older Worker* suggests principles of adult, and specifically older-adult, education that need to be considered in HRD programming, as well as specific types of content and action planning ideas for learning sessions.

A fourth audience that will benefit from this book is one consisting of those who conduct education, training, and development for two kinds of clients: small businesses that do not have an HRD department, and adult educators in the nonprofit or public sectors whose activities are directed primarily toward older adults, especially those seeking to reenter the job market. *The Older Worker* can assist these trainers and educators in designing and conducting meaningful, relevant programming. The benefits mentioned above for HRD practitioners apply to this group.

A fifth audience that will find the book helpful is that of persons engaged in academic pursuits in colleges and universities. Faculty in departments of management, human resource development, adult education, gerontology, and human development can use it in their instruction. It will be useful to them for its information and ideas about older persons not only as employees in corporations, but also as their own students, staff, and faculty. The book can be used to special advantage in interdisciplinary courses, as it stimulates thinking on such issues as what management styles are most suitable to older employees, and what is the best way to facilitate career development in later life.

Overview of the Contents

Chapters One through Three take an issue-centered approach to flexible, imaginative, and sensitive use of older workers in the context of changing demographics. Chapter One poses four key questions of concern and responds to them. These questions are:

1. Why do we need a new emphasis on older-worker employment?
2. What beliefs have hindered older-worker employment?
3. What can older workers contribute to the organization?
4. What do some companies who have used older workers have to say?

Chapter Two focuses on specific demographic and organizational trends that will affect the adoption of older-worker policies and strategies. In so doing, it presents three issues for consideration to managers, especially HRD managers:

1. What kinds of practices do human resource professionals and older workers suggest be considered?
2. What are some of the specific trends impacting human resource programming for older workers?
3. What employee-specific concerns are impacting human resource programming for older workers?

In Chapter Three, I explain just who this unique human resource, the older worker, really is. This chapter directs attention to the issues about which department managers of older workers, as well as HRD professionals, need to have knowledge and understanding to more appropriately carry out their jobs. The questions offered and responded to here are:

1. What does it mean to be "old" in America?
2. What might an older worker be feeling and experiencing?
3. How can an unwanted retirement affect an older person's self-image and social standing?

Chapters Four, Five, and Six provide an inverted pyramid of information about older-worker policies, practices, and programs in corporations. It is inverted because the discussion moves from broad consideration of "packages" of older worker practices and programs in Chapter Four, to brief case studies demonstrating the operation of these packages in Chapter Five, to more detailed exposition of learning programs, specifically for older workers, in Chapter Six. Examples of alternative work options and other adjustments to traditional company practice such as part-time and temporary work, job redesign, education and training to retain or return older workers to the staff, preparation for next career, and wellness programming are offered in Chapter Four. Building on this overview, Chapter Five shows how nine companies have responded to issues they faced related to older workers. Chapter Six narrows the field of emphasis still further to literature and corporate practice on learning design for older workers and explores ideas about what learning *process* may work best for them.

Career development for older workers is the crux of Chapter Seven. As people live longer and experience developmental changes in life and work, a sizable percentage of them are likely to seek opportunities in career fields beyond the parameters of their present company and vocation. Examples of companies that have implemented career development for older employees are presented. I outline a six-stage serial career planning model that is especially useful for older persons because it draws on their actual life experience and also depends on it for successful activation and use.

As a multigenerational work force evolves, managers will need to develop appropriate sensitivities and skills. Chapter Eight introduces some of these issues, for example, those related to the older worker–younger manager dynamic, to establishing a climate conducive to motivating the mature employee, and to the particular stresses the older worker may encounter, especially as he or she takes part in an HRD program. In each of these areas, I offer specific ideas about how managers can effectively attend to these matters and thereby cultivate the potential of their older subordinates. The second part of Chapter Eight suggests program content for management training and education.

Special consideration is given in Chapter Nine to issues related to the increasing numbers and significance of older women in the work force.* This chapter clarifies the special needs, problems, and opportunities of older women in a changing economy. Concerns unique to them center around the likelihood that they will experience at least two of the three great biases in this culture: ageism, sexism, and racism (older black women encounter all three). Moreover, family concerns have had a dramatic effect on their financial status, for example, with regard to a possible lack of continuity in work history, and responsibilities in later life for an elderly parent. What HRD can do for this large group, and what specific learning programs are needed for them, is treated.

Chapter Ten looks at action planning for older-worker issues in three areas: for the organization, for the manager, and for the employee under the manager's leadership and facilitation. Finally, in an appendix titled "Resources for Further Information," I provide an organizational resource section for the manager who wishes to be up-to-date and involved in older-worker issues and a section on publications divided into topical

---

*In other chapters, except as mentioned, the problems of older women and men are treated together. However, rather than use the awkward "he or she" and "him or her," as no inclusive pronoun has been generally adopted, I have in some instances varied the gender of the pronoun, thus giving approximately equal attention to female and male.

areas of interest for managers. This reading list includes some more specialized subjects — such as compensation and benefits, age discrimination, and so on — with which a manager may wish to become familiar.

Acknowledgments

Many individuals and organizations deserve credit and thanks for their assistance in the writing of *The Older Worker*. I owe special appreciation to Len and Zeace Nadler for their ongoing encouragement and sound advice. I might not have made it to this point without them. For their time, courtesy, and information, I am grateful to Bill St. Clair of McDonald's Corporation, Dean Hewitt of the National Council on the Aging's Prime Time Productivity Program, Bernard Nash of the Division of Business Partnerships of the American Association of Retired Persons, Janice Davidson of the association's National Gerontology Resource Center, and Beverly Frailey, formerly reference librarian at National-Louis University. For her diligence and fortitude in assisting with the word processing and editing of the manuscript for this book, a thank you to Eleanor Clark.

Note to the Reader: I would be most interested in hearing from corporations and nonprofit and public sector agencies that are maintaining, establishing, or expanding programs for older workers. For a possible second edition of this book, material on what is being done for workers age fifty and over who are still employed in a company, as well as retired workers who have returned to the firm, is wanted and needed. I especially welcome input from organizations that have placed older employees in a management track.

Lombard, Illinois   Noreen Hale
July 1990

The Author

Noreen Hale is director of program development at National-Louis University (previously National College of Education). She received her B.A. degree from Hunter College of the City University of New York in political science, her M.A. degree from the University of San Francisco in political science and history, and her Ed.D. degree from Indiana University in adult education.

Her professional experience includes being manager of a community relations department in a hospital providing community education programming for older adults; director of a government-funded program to design and conduct train-the-trainer sessions in gerontology for mental health staff working with elderly clients; consultant for adult and geriatric programs at a community mental health center; and consultant for career and job search for displaced older workers at a college center for older adults. She teaches "Introduction to Aging in America" to undergraduate and graduate students at National-Louis University.

Hale's major areas of interest and study have centered on the older worker, women's life development, educating women (especially older women) for management roles, and facilitating the personal and professional growth of students who reenter higher education at midlife and later. She has published articles and papers on the relationship between gerontology, management, and education, including "Applying Adult Education Principles to Mental Health Care of the Aged" (1981), "You're Only Old Twice: Retraining and Re-Careering for Older Workers" (1987), "Managing a 'Graying' Workforce" (1988), "Meeting the Educational Needs of Mature Women Students to Be Effective Managers" (1988), and "Growing Old: Seven Women, Seven Views" in *Women, Aging and Ageism* (1990), edited by Evelyn Rosenthal.

The Older Worker

Chapter 1

The Growing
Emphasis on
Older Workers

Anticipating and planning labor needs was not a priority concern in the United States until quite recently. There had always been a ready supply of housewives and youth to call upon either in peak periods in a given company's business year or during national crises, such as war. Now that the supply of younger workers is decreasing for demographic reasons and the women who used to participate in the work force on a casual basis are fully employed, companies are beginning to acknowledge that they will need to make better use of the employees they already have. A sizable portion of these is made up of "older" workers.

A Boston University study has estimated that by the year 2010 workers over age fifty-five could constitute more than 25 percent of the work force (Memmott, 1986). Several other similar estimates could be cited. It is valuable, then, to look at why companies use older workers and how they assess their efforts. With the expansion of the service sector, there is a growing realization in, for example, the fast food industry that the new hires may be older adults. As early as August 4, 1987, the Petersburg, Virginia, *Progress Index,* in a front-page article, described how corporations were becoming more aware of the need for accommodating mature employees and incorporating them into employee ranks. The same article quoted Catherine Fyock, director of field services for Kentucky Fried Chicken: "When you realize there will be 20 percent fewer teenagers in 1990 than there were in 1975, you know you are going to have to do something to fill those jobs." For Fyock, that something involved hiring mature workers. Similarly, Pam Farr, personnel manager at J. W. Marriott Corporation, remarked in the same article that employing more older Americans was going to be the "national business strategy of the 1990s." Consideration of this strategy, however, can be highly problematic. Let us review some of the reasons why.

How Old is "Older"?

To speak of "older-worker" issues is itself a problem. There is widespread variation in how "older" is defined in law, theories, surveys, studies, and the popular press and media. "Older" can be a label attached to anyone from forty to seventy and beyond. For the purposes of this study, age fifty will be considered as the entry point into later adulthood in the private and public sectors of employment. This age provides a point of overlap between those still employed and those who may have left, then reentered the work force in second, third, or fourth careers. Karp suggests that there may be a "changing age consciousness" that begins at or around age fifty, "an age that strongly carries the connotation of being at a mid-point," of having lived for half a century, so that "age becomes less a stranger and more an intimate" (1988, pp. 727, 730, 729).

It will be important to remember, however, that the studies cited in this book often vary in their definitions. One article may discuss older workers and use age forty-five as the demarcation point between young and old, while another may imply age fifty-five or sixty. As age fifty or over is the designation used for "older worker" in this book, the term includes two categories of employee: (1) the preretirement worker, and (2) the retiree from a company who has reentered the work force. Because of the widespread prevalence and popularity of early retirement, most of the information in this book concerns the second group.

Yet another caveat involves the connotation of the term *human resource development* (HRD) and its main activities, training, education, and development. I am using Nadler and Nadler's definitions of these terms. Human resource development consists of "organized learning experiences provided by employers within a specified period of time to bring about the possibility of performance improvement and/or personal growth" (1989, p. 4). In the context of this book, I define training as providing formal assistance so that employees can do the same job better, for example, by having their keyboard skills updated after coming out of retirement. I treat training as learning focused on the employee's *current* job and education as preparation for a *future* job. Development concerns personal growth but is not job-focused. Again, it is important to keep in mind that the authors cited here may employ these and other such terms differently.

Older Workers in a New Perspective

Why should HRD managers concern themselves with the older worker? Of course, several trends in the mass media have operated to create an interest. Articles in the popular press such as *Time* magazine, TV sitcoms like " The Golden Girls," and TV news programs and documentaries, as well as movies like *On Golden Pond* and *Cocoon,* have made the nation more conscious of its aging population in general. At the same time, a cost-conscious business sector is becoming increasingly aware of two developments: the expense of paying for benefits over many years and providing early retirement incentive packages, and the fact that in the near future the majority of its employees will be middle-aged.

Demographics portend an older work force with fewer young people available for entry-level positions. Federal legislation against age discrimination in employment has also made industry look more closely at age-related personnel policies and practices. With greater attention directed to the older segment of the work force, companies are finding concern for their older employees valuable not only from a humanistic standpoint but also for the sake of public relations. Still another reason is that the burgeoning literature in the field of aging and employment has allowed some long-standing but seldom discussed issues to come out of the closet. Among these issues are whether the older worker is worth the investment to retrain and how productive and cost-effective a graying work force can really be.

Works of the mid to late 1980s (for example, Rosen and Jerdee, 1985c; Sandell, 1987; Dennis, 1988) issued a call to action and urged corporate America to assume a more active stance with regard to older-worker programs. They proposed that corporations be creative and assertive in enhancing and extending the work life of their older employees. Moreover, they provided specific examples of progressive human resource policies including:

- *A philosophy of reinvesting in older workers* through education and training
- *Cultivation of more empathic interpersonal skills,* such as active listening, by younger managers especially
- *Maintaining workers but placing them in less physically demanding roles* such as word processor
- *Costing out the actual benefit-detriment ratio of using older workers* and developing appropriate cost-management strategies rather than making unfounded assumptions based on misinformation and fear
- *Stressing the increments with age* such as experience, loyalty to the employer, maturity in decision making and problem solving, and accumulated knowledge and dependability

All of these activities involve information that can be disseminated through HRD learning programs.

In the December 1987 issue of *The Aging Workforce,* several noted persons involved in older-worker issues offered thoughtful and provocative opinions. Former secretary of labor, William Brock, under whose leadership the department's Workforce 2000 Project began, stated why individual companies as well as the nation as a whole need older workers: "They have the skill, the dedication, the loyalty, and the experience to make our businesses and our country productive" (p. 2). Daniel Knowles, vice-president for human resources planning at the Grumman

Corporation, concurred with Brock's statement, maintaining that although the middle-aged and older segments of the work force are both the cornerstone groups of society and industry and also the most sizable ones, they are often, ironically, the most neglected. He identified a baseline commitment of industry to the older worker (p. 4):

1. Formulate an equitable policy for older workers and make the policy known to all employees.
2. Make sure that a statement of the above policy is included in all supervisory education programs.
3. Take an inventory of existing personnel policies and practices to eliminate inherent biases.
4. Conduct an age audit of personnel and compare this against information available through the Department of Labor.
5. Establish fair standards and mechanisms for evaluating age discrimination cases.

William Kohlberg, president of the National Alliance of Business, admonished corporate America in this same issue of *The Aging Workforce* (p. 5) not to be lax or procrastinate in developing state-of-the-art policies with regard to older workers. The demographic projection that 25 percent of Americans will be over fifty years of age early in the twenty-first century, Kohlberg remarked, "will spell trouble for American businesses if they continue their present hiring and retiring policies."

Combating Myths and Stereotypes

Companies' actions with regard to older employees may have their origin in beliefs about the latter's attitudes and capabilities and also about changes that take place as people age. McConnell (1984, p. 18) contends that age discrimination, originally subscribed to by pockets of industry, spread to the larger society after 1915. As he describes the diffusion, "the youth cult of the 1920s and the high unemployment of the depression era turned older workers into a convenient scapegoat." The older worker, believed to be in inevitable decline, was a handy target in an era of rapid technological advance and a new emphasis on speed, efficiency, and adaptability. By then, the mature employee was considered ineffectual and expendable. In the late 1920s, approximately 20 percent of companies used physical exams to screen workers. These exams often were not directly related to job performance but were used instead to eliminate "outmoded" employees, who tended to be older.

Results of an investigation by the Labor Department in the 1920s showed that age bias was widespread in the nation and needed to be addressed by legislation. Subsequently, Congress passed the Age Discrimination in Employment Act (ADEA) of 1967 and its later amendments.

Lawrence, in her 1988 study of socially generated age effects in an electric utility, suggests it is the beliefs shared by the organization's personnel about what happens to people as they age in a work environment that produce age norms for an organization. These norms, in turn, have a direct and often adverse impact on managerial behavior toward the older employee. If, for example, the prevailing false perception in a company is that workers automatically become demotivated as they age, a manager may not expend the effort to devise appropriate rewards for older workers. Moreover, Lee and Clemons (1985), using simulated employment decisions, found that favorable decisions about mature employees tended to be made when one or both of the following factors were present: (1) the choice in question was *not* between an older or younger worker, and (2) information about the older employee, stated in terms of objective performance criteria, was made available to the decision maker. Therefore, if a manager did not have to make a knowingly age-based choice, she tended to make a more positive judgment about the older worker.

Throughout the evolution of age bias in the workplace, the persistence of myths about older workers has complicated the matter. Jean Scher, senior employment specialist of the Atlanta, Georgia, Regional Commission (Hall and Wessel, 1986), has identified seven basic myths that encourage age-biased behavior in those who believe them, namely, that older workers:

1. Are not as productive as younger persons
2. Are more expensive for the employer to retrain in the sense that they have a limited future with the company
3. Cost the employer more in health insurance and other benefits
4. Have problematic interpersonal relations with co-workers
5. Would prefer to coast until retirement
6. Have high rates of absenteeism and are accident-prone
7. Are all in good shape financially

The U.S. Department of Health and Human Services' Administration on Aging (AOA) also singled out these inaccurate beliefs for rebuttal in its publication *Older Workers: Myths and Reality* (1986). Its responses to the myths mentioned above are condensed here.

Productivity. The AOA contends that there is no decline in productivity with age. As far back as 1978, Sonnenfeld pointed out that the experiences of companies that had never had an age limit in hiring or maintaining workers showed that older employees could perform as well as or better than younger ones. A 1985 Yankelovich survey showed that one of the positive impressions received by managers of older workers was that they were productive. However, the perceptions that older workers could be hard to motivate and were inflexible were found to be more relevant to the managers' overall opinion of older workers (American Association of Retired Persons, 1985a).

Cost in Training. According to the AOA, little reason exists to support this belief. Cost-effective training and education need to be developed for all age groups.

Cost in Benefits. The Travelers Corporation conducted a study on this topic that indicated it is unsafe to assume that older workers are more expensive employees simply because they are older. While the costs of some benefits (for instance, health and life insurance) do increase as a person ages, other benefits are linked more with seniority and salary.

Interpersonal Relations. The AOA points out that older workers rank as high or higher than younger workers in terms of interpersonal skills.

Waiting for Retirement. Because older adults are so diverse, the idea that older employees may be coasting until retirement is a gross overgeneralization. Among a few of the factors that influence such an attitude are the availability of alternative work opportunities, what meaning work holds in the individual's life, and whether retirement income is judged to be sufficient.

Proneness to Accidents and Absenteeism. With reference to accidents, the AOA pamphlet points out that although older workers make up about 13.6 percent of the labor force, they account for only 9.7 percent of workplace injuries. It is, however, true that when older workers are injured, it takes them longer to recover. As far as absenteeism is concerned, older workers show up for work as often or more frequently than do those in other age groups.

Financial Condition. Although there have been notable improvements in the economic situation of older workers since about 1970, one in seven people aged sixty-five and older lives in poverty. People can work and not suffer the loss of Social Security benefits only if they adhere to the so-called retirement test, which limits earnings. The AOA also reports that many older workers have said they would prefer to continue working, and would be willing to modify their hours and the nature of their work despite their desire to continue in a similar type of job (American Association of Retired Persons, 1988a).

What Older Workers Can Do

In *The Aging Worker: Research and Recommendations* (1983), Doering, Rhodes, and Schuster concluded that the employment of older workers is consonant with organizational effectiveness. There are various positive traits that these and other students of industrial gerontology attribute to mature employees. Robinson (1983, p. 70) asserts that "training of older workers is actually a good investment." She points to the fact that they are more likely, once retrained, to stay with the company than are younger employees. She also cites studies suggesting that older employees tend to have lower rates of turnover and as good as, if not better, attendance records. Further, Robinson refers to the U.S. Senate report of 1977, which described an analysis of the quantity and quality of work of more than three thousand managerial, office, industrial, and retail employees who were over sixty years of age. The results showed that they performed as well as or more effectively than younger workers. The value of experience to an organization is also affirmed by Lazarus and Lauer (1985), who contend that the older person may be a better problem solver because of his or her longer history of coping with life's vicissitudes.

Humple and Lyons (1983) maintain that there are differences among younger, middle-aged, and older persons in terms of their values concerning work. They identify several factors that they found to be particularly characteristic of the older worker:

- Stronger sense of loyalty and commitment
- More emphasis on quality of work life than on work itself
- Economic motives that may decrease at least to the point where earnings from work are seen to supplement income
- Desire for less than full-time work so that work is seen as part of daily life rather than its focal point
- More emphasis on social and personal concerns such as being with friends or feeling appreciated or recognized
- Greater pride in craftsmanship or in the quality of work
- A greater attempt to work harder to make up for self-perceived failures or inadequacies
- A deeper sense of the work ethic of giving one's employer a good day's work and believing that work is intrinsically valuable

Lazarus and Lauer (1985, p. 58) concur with several of these observations and note, "The message . . . is that older workers have a decidedly stronger work ethic and more positive attitude toward work than their younger counterparts."

Peterson (1983, p. 67) discusses various characteristics of older workers that HRD managers and educators in general need to take into account in developing programs for them. In reviewing the literature on intelligence and performance, he concludes, "Even beyond age seventy, few people are so rigid or so restricted in neurological functioning that they cannot learn when they choose to. The clear message of the literature on intelligence is that there is little reason for hesitation in attempting to teach persons of any age." Accordingly, in evaluating what appear to be learning declines in older workers, it is important for managers to be aware that other factors such as loss of vision or hearing, general fatigue, or even a faster-paced work tempo may contribute to or even cause abrupt declines in performance. Moreover, managers should realize that the company has some degree of control even over performance changes brought about by physical decline. Most of the physical problems Peterson refers to — for example, slower reaction time and lowered energy levels — can be addressed creatively by looking at them as opportunities and challenges.

Doering, Rhodes, and Schuster (1983) call attention to the fact that older workers tend to manifest greater overall satisfaction — satisfaction with the job, with working conditions, and with supervision. These researchers acknowledge a direct correlation between the actual policies and practices of companies and their employees' behaviors and attitudes. Therefore, if employers want to understand the lack of career orientation or motivation sometimes attributed to older workers, they need to view these factors as part of their corporate culture, especially its values and norms.

Developing Older Workers

In the light of so much evidence that older adults do retain the capacity to learn, Doering, Rhodes, and Schuster advise employers to assess and adapt learning methods in relation to the needs and characteristics of the age group in question.

Companies also need to review interview and performance appraisal practices to determine whether and to what degree age bias is present and what form it takes. They should consider whether their current practices validly measure older workers' capabilities and performance. Part of the HRD function, then, may be to educate managers about what these capabilities are and what kinds of instruments can measure them appropriately.

In developing compensation, pension, benefits, and retirement packages HRD should also take into consideration that the values and preferences of older workers may differ from those of younger ones. For example, depending on their financial condition, education, and job satisfaction, quality-of-life issues may be paramount for older workers. Education about life development and career stages would be useful for personnel engaged in the development of such packages.

Because nontraditional career paths are no longer unusual, a person may enter a completely different line of work later in life. Therefore, career paths and career ladders should be designed to suit the needs of specific age groups. In particular, as the public is increasingly aware, women workers with young children need more job flexibility, and employers must look more closely at developing varied opportunities in this area. Some of these job options could also be extended to older workers to make better use of their talents and skills. Such programs would be more effectively designed and implemented if managers were taught about alternative patterns of work and their benefits for various groups.

If worker obsolescence is a problem, then concrete steps should be taken to avoid it, especially in high technology industries. These steps might well include a stated and adhered-to commitment by top management to a policy of reinvesting in its older employees. The policy could be implemented through ongoing training and education, and by equipping workers with multiple skills so that they cannot easily become outmoded.

As for the physical problems of older workers, Doering, Rhodes, and Schuster recommend that, wherever possible, companies use state-of-the-art technology to reduce the physically demanding aspects of their jobs and assist them in learning new skills. Policymakers should take into consideration the relativity of age as a concept; *chronological age,* the most common benchmark, is incomplete and often inaccurate as a predictor of performance and productivity. In the opinion of these researchers, there are at least four other kinds of age. The classifications they mention are *anatomical age, physiological age, pathological age,* and *psychological age.* Managers must keep the relativity (and heterogeneity) of age in mind when supervising and developing learning programs for all workers. For example, all aging persons cannot be lumped into the same category. One can be "old" at forty in terms of being psychologically or emotionally dull or because of a pathological condition. On the other hand, a seventy-year-old could be considered "young" in the sense of emotional openness, spontaneity, and receptivity to new ideas (American Association of Retired Persons, 1985b, 1986b, 1986e).

Older-Worker Programs: The Bottom Line

Not all companies have been slow to adopt programs for older workers, and some have had them long enough to assess their results. Paul (1987) surveyed companies that adopted alternative work arrangements for older workers from the mid 1960s to the early 1980s. The portion of her analysis devoted to organizations that actively recruited older workers singled out four reasons why they had opted to do so:

1. They believed that older workers would attract older consumers.
2. They wanted to meet affirmative action guidelines.
3. They expected that older workers could and would be role models for younger employees in work ethic and dedication.
4. They acknowledged a need to gain experience with older employees because demographics pointed to an older work force in the future.

According to Paul, managers also noted, though to a far lesser degree than the previous four reasons, that older persons were useful because they appeared to be more content with entry-level positions. In general, companies tended to hire older workers when it helped their financial and public image. Prevailing business conditions were generally the deciding factor as to if and when they hired or retained them.

Approximately 75 percent of the employers queried in the Yankelovich survey (American Association of Retired Persons, 1985a) asserted that the strong points of older employees were that they were:

- Productive and efficient
- Cost-effective (90 percent of employers cited this factor)
- Committed to the work ethic
- Loyal and dedicated to the company's goals and objectives
- Role models
- Capable of successfully completing retraining
- Interested and task-oriented

The Travelers Corporation, in the vanguard of hiring older workers, has been especially interested in utilizing its retirees. Retiring workers sign up to be part of a job bank. As the need arises, they are retrained either for positions related to their previous experience (for example, someone with keyboard skills might be trained to use a computer) or for jobs that are completely new to them. According to Harold E. Johnson, senior vice-president of personnel and administration, "The Travelers believes that retirees are an important part of the work force, and that they are willing and eager to learn how to use the latest technology" (Retirement Advisors, 1988, p. 1).

Tim Warren, president of Warren Publishing Company in Boston, has posed a challenging question to corporate America (Goddard, 1987): Why should a company make a productive employee stop working at a specific age when it can provide an environment that will help that employee remain productive? Gerald Maguire, vice-president of corporate services for Bankers Life and Casualty Company, reported as far back as 1977 to one of the House Subcommittees on Aging on his company's positive experience with older workers; he acknowledged their dependability, attendance, job tenure, and productivity (Jacobson, 1980).

James Challenger, president of Challenger, Gray, and Christmas, Inc., an outplacement firm in Chicago, has predicted that companies will become increasingly more amenable to hiring older workers as they grow in awareness that such workers are likely to stay with the company after training as long and longer than younger ones. He points out that a present-day corporate myth is that if a company invests in a twenty-three-year-old, that person will stay and grow with the company; given today's mobile society, this is unlikely (Retirement Advisors, 1988).

Chapters Four and Five will consider in more detail what organizations have to say about their experience with older-worker programs. Meanwhile, Chapter Two shows why these programs will become necessary as both the for-profit and the not-for-profit sectors are challenged by major changes in the work force during the years to come.

Chapter 2

Meeting the
Challenge of an
Aging Work Force

Managers do not function in a vacuum. They are regularly boosted or buffeted by environmental factors — economic, social, legal, and so on — that affect how they perform their jobs, and how well. In particular, they need to be sensitive and responsive to the evolving demographic profile of America's work force and to the new patterns that will emerge in the year 2000 and beyond. Let us review some of the more significant changes that can be anticipated.

In an increasingly globalized marketplace, the new work force will be multicultural in nature. It will be necessary for selection, staffing, and human resource planning to reflect these changes. Women, minorities (especially blacks), and immigrants (especially Hispanics and Asians) will constitute 80–90 percent of new entrants into the labor market. Only 15–20 percent of net additions to the labor force between 1985 and 2000 will be white males.

By the year 2000, according to the National Conference on the Nation's Workforce, Year 2000, three-fifths of all women over age sixteen will be employed (*Workforce 2000, Executive Summary . . .*, 1988). They will, however, be functioning in a workplace environment still based on a societal model in which men worked and women stayed at home. This patriarchal package includes such human resource policies as those related to pay, fringe benefits, and pensions.

The same source estimates that there will be fewer young adults to assume entry-level positions; the pool of available youth

15

will decline from its current level of 30 percent to 16 percent. The median age of the work force by 2000 will be approximately forty vis-à-vis thirty-four in the early 1980s. Workers over forty, who now total 43 million, will increase in number to 56 million by 1996. The proportion of such older adults in the population is increasing at a faster rate than that of any other age group and many pre-retirees have said they would prefer to continue working. HRD managers face the prospect of handling a glut of employees in the age range from thirty-five to fifty-four — the aging baby boomers — with fewer possible positions into which they can move.

For many retirees and companies, early retirement has not proven the panacea it was assumed to be. It is costly in terms of both lost talent and financial outlay. Yet, should the trend to early departure from the work force continue, the traditional retirement age by the year 2000 will be around fifty-nine. Companies must address a gerontological imperative predicted by the Bureau of the Census: by the year 2020, one in three persons in the population will be over age fifty-five. *Trends and Issues Alert,* a publication of the National Center for Research in Vocational Education, maintains that these adults are capable of productive employment for an additional fifteen to twenty-five years ("Older Workers," 1988). This is especially true if they receive company-supported in-house or contracted-out training, retraining, and career counseling for the more specialized and higher-level skilled jobs of the next century.

The larger societal framework in which corporations will assume a more proactive stance with regard to the older worker is also one that illustrates how important demographics are going to be. While in 1980 there were approximately five workers to every nonworker, by 2030 that ratio will have been reduced to three to one (American Association of Retired Persons, 1987). The AARP also estimates that the number of workers for every Social Security beneficiary is likely to decline from 3.7 in 1981 to 2.2 in 2030, placing a financially draining burden on those in the work force.

For all these reasons, then, it behooves companies to begin looking at ways of enhancing the productive capacity of their mature employees. *Working Age,* a publication of the AARP's Worker Equity Department, cites a review by Waldman and

Avolio of prior research on age and productivity ("Productivity Increases . . . ," 1986) suggesting that performance levels actually increase as employees get older. Since many older males are currently employed in manufacturing, where there is a greater likelihood that they will be displaced by automation and because their skills are obsolete, and older women are frequently functioning in low-skilled service and trade arenas, there is significant potential for training and education. Persons over age fifty are also capable of assuming managerial and executive roles and would need to be educated for these types of positions too. Initiatives by companies are needed to match the desire for continued employment by older adults, a desire encouraged by some reduction in 1990 in the earnings limitation imposed with regard to Social Security benefits.

What HRD Professionals Recommend — and Older Workers Want

Currently, HRD directors appear to be in the vanguard of those corporate leaders who both recognize the need for more enlightened practices, including HRD activities, concerning older employees and lament the lack of them. In an analysis ("Major Survey Report . . . ," 1988) of a survey of 600 HR managers conducted under the aegis of the American Society for Personnel Administration (ASPA) and the Commerce Clearing House, Rosen and Jerdee noted the discrepancy between the preferences of those surveyed and actual company practices. Managers seemed to attribute the disaffection of middle-aged-to-older workers, the "marking time" phenomenon, and career plateauing to the corporations themselves, which had failed to implement relevant career development, job redesign, and learning programs. The two older-worker policies most often identified by the managers were job transfer, mentioned by 46 percent, and an annual training needs assessment, mentioned by 38 percent (p. 3). Ironically, the survey's results showed that training needs were not necessarily being met by the measures being taken for that purpose. Rosen and Jerdee contend that managers who support older-worker programs need to argue for them in terms of the bottom line. They need to collect financial data that will demonstrate to their organizations the high cost of *not* addressing the concerns of middle-aged and older workers.

Under the auspices of the AARP, the Gallup organization conducted a poll eventually published as *Work and Retirement: Employees over 40 and Their Views* (American Association of Retired Persons, 1986d). This report summarized findings of a survey of 1,300 full-time workers over forty years of age, including a subsample of those aged sixty-three and older. Employees in the age range from fifty to sixty-two most often cited economic reasons, especially the need to maintain benefits, for continuing to work. The subsample leaned toward the nature of the work itself and the enjoyment derived from it as a preference. Among the lowest-rated reasons for remaining at work were opportunity for promotion and growth in the job. The latter issue should serve as a prompt to corporations to re-examine their philosophy of investment in older workers. If a worker of any age feels that there is little chance of advancement within his or her organization, that worker is likely to become demotivated.

Job training is another area considered in the AARP–Gallup study. Here again there is a gap between estimated need and actual practice. Two out of three workers received on-the-job training within three years of having been surveyed, generally to upgrade skills. The kind of training varied, however, depending on age and other factors. For example, private sector organizations as a whole provided less training to persons aged sixty-three and over, the less educated, persons at lower echelons of the organization, and those who were paid less.

Interestingly, in contrast to the managerial perception to be discussed in later chapters, approximately 40 percent of the mature employees expressed a desire to upgrade their current skills. Another 45 percent of those questioned wanted training to prepare them for a different job, or for work completely unrelated to their current career (pp. 11–12). Fully one-third of workers reported they would postpone retirement if they could earn increased pension or Social Security benefits.

Existing policies, however, encourage early retirement and offer insufficient or no incentives to stay employed. The adoption of more flexible work arrangements—for example, part-time or shared jobs, as are described in Chapter Four—would enable companies to maintain valued employees and address the stated preference of numerous preretirees to continue working. Morrison (1983) cites several barriers to older-worker employment. Among these are age bias, lack of appropriate job opportunities, discouragement in searching for work, and perceived health problems. For example, a prospective employer may make the unwarranted assumption that someone over age fifty is likely to be in ill health. Or a corporate interviewer, because of stereotypical beliefs, may read lack of motivation into an older job applicant's responses.

Matching Skills to Demand

Managers face a formidable but exciting challenge in matching people and jobs in the future. Whether the prospective employee is over fifty, a female of any age, or a member of a racial or ethnic minority, HRD managers will have to train, educate, and develop this person in the context of a rapidly changing workplace landscape. Included in the trends affecting the environment in which HRD managers will function are those identified in the Hudson Institute's report, *Workforce 2000: Work and Workers for the Twenty-First Century* (Johnston and Packer, 1987):

1. While manufacturing will play a smaller role in the economy, the growth of the service sector will escalate and will generate most new wealth.
2. The new occupational mix will increase job prospects in professional, managerial, technical, sales, and service areas.
3. New jobs in these fields will require greater education and training as well as higher skill levels. The Hudson Institute projects that about one-third of the new positions to be created by the year 2000 will require an undergraduate degree or more. This stands in sharp contrast to the current work force, in which only about one-fifth of all occupations necessitate one having an undergraduate degree.
4. The pressing need for increased productivity in the service sector may lead to two developments: higher levels of em-

ployment for those with high levels of skill, sophistication, and education, and less employment for those without.

While U.S. academic institutions must address the complex needs of an increasingly diversified, global, and multicultural economy through relevant curricula, HRD departments must also be prepared to fill in the gaps between a given organization's requirements and the competencies of those who work or want to work in it. Within the past twenty years, job growth in the service sector has supported the hiring of workers who are low-paid, have low-level skills, and who may be marginally productive. Growing demand for increased output per worker in fields such as health care, finance, retailing, and government will impel further automation of work and downsizing of work units. With such workplace adjustments, it is likely that low-skill workers will be at a serious occupational disadvantage. Of particular concern is the likelihood that perhaps millions of new workers may lack even rudimentary skills. Thus HRD managers face not only an opportunity for affirmative action by constructively integrating these workers into the organization, but also for prolonging the work lives of older workers who, despite the myths, are able to learn and learn well.

This may prove to be a crucial change for HRD managers. After the year 2000, changes in manufacturing technology such as CAD (computer assisted design) and CAM (computer assisted manufacturing) could displace workers, including numerous older workers, in the durable goods field especially. A worker's holding his or her own in the face of the advance of CAD/CAM may depend on the available chances for learning, as well as the willingness of workers to become educated in manipulating robots and in handling digitally controlled machine tools and automated materials handling systems. "Workers of any age who are to prevail in the face of modern workplace technology will be those whose skills remain pertinent to the tasks at hand" ("CAD/CAM and the Older Worker," 1988).

Matching Programs to People

HRD managers must cultivate not only an awareness of the environmental factors affecting their own organizations but also of the employee-specific issues — the "people" factors — influencing the philosophy and operations of their departments. Five of these issues are dealt with here (see Table 1).

Shifting Values. Oldenburg in a *Washington Post* article (1988) has called attention to the shift of values in today's lean-and-mean workplace. This shift reflects the fact that between 1981 and 1986 approximately 10.8 million workers lost jobs due to mergers, acquisitions, plant shutdowns, closings, and layoffs, and that about 50 percent of these jobs were lost permanently (Fraze, 1988).

The late 1980s, as Oldenburg describes the situation, had been an employer's market. At that time, companies pressured by economic exigencies to streamline personnel and tighten budgets and expenditures took a hard line toward employees who were, essentially, viewed as "commodities." As a result, the unwritten but traditionally acknowledged psychological contract between an employer who provides security and rewards in exchange for an employee's loyalty and willingness to sacrifice appears to have undergone a renegotiation. Many employers define the new contract as a transactional model of a fair day's work for a fair day's pay, rather than as a relational one of mutual faithfulness and support. Similarly, employees, especially of the baby-boom generation and younger, affirm a reciprocal contract in which, given the decreasing paternalism of companies, they have the concomitant right to change jobs and even careers, and to move elsewhere if the pay or the quality of work life is better.

Moreover, there appear to be clear value differences between workers above and under age fifty. Younger employees, according to Oldenburg, reflect the 1960s orientation of distrust

Table 1. Factors Affecting Organizational Relations with Older Workers.

1.   Shifting values
2.   ADEA
3.   Opportunities for training
4.   Alternative work options
5.   Top management commitment

of authority, while older workers believe they will be treated equitably if they do their jobs. Fraze illustrates this tendency by observing that even when employees, especially those over fifty or older, are notified that their plant will close, they tend as a group to perform quality work to the end. While one motivation for this behavior is to secure pension and severance rights, "mostly they like to feel . . . that someone in the upper management of the firm cares enough about them to tell them in time to prepare for the worst" (p. 49). Older workers schooled in the Protestant ethic of hard work consider work a duty. Younger co-workers, on the other hand, may seek fulfillment in their work. The two segments also viewed opportunity for advancement differently. Mature employees expected promotions to be a reward for seniority and experience. This was in marked contrast to their younger colleagues, who expected a rapid rise up the career ladder based on the merit of their performance. Thus, HRD managers will need to capitalize on the skills and dedication of current older workers and, at the same time, anticipate the shifting needs and differing values of the formerly young workers as they age.

The Age Discrimination in Employment Act (ADEA). The value contrast between generations is also likely to manifest itself in their dealing with age discrimination. While some workers in the aforementioned AARP–Gallup survey of employees over age forty contended that they experienced age discrimination, the reasons most often given for not taking action were that it would not do any good and they did not want to make waves. Since the passage of the Age Discrimination in Employment Act in 1967, the number of claims filed with state agencies and the Equal Employment Opportunity Commission (EEOC) have more than doubled. One reason for this is that since the legislation defines the "older worker" as aged forty or over, it affects the baby boomers, who are, as a group, more assertive about their rights. Owing to this liberal definition by the ADEA, the coming saturation of the labor supply by aging baby boomers, especially in midlevel management positions, and possible greater enforcement of the act by government, HRD managers need not only a general acquaintance with its provisions but also to make sure their companies' policies and practices are in compliance with it. Sometimes the age bias in corporate practice may be subtle. For example, encouragement of early retirement with the golden handshake of attractive payments may mask discouragement of an older worker's remaining with the company so that he or she can be replaced by younger — and cheaper — blood.

Opportunities for Training. Related to the more insidious aspects of age discrimination is the security of retraining opportunities for workers over age fifty. According to Fraze (1988), of the workers displaced by the takeovers and closings so prevalent in the 1980s, older job seekers were those who took the greatest amount of time to find new employment, often at lower pay, or who were locked out of the labor supply permanently. While official government figures show a lower rate of unemployment for older workers, these do not encompass the ones who became so disheartened in the job search that they simply gave up.

Fraze (p. 46) also reports that the "lack of adequate training to survive in an increasingly technological society" is the single major problem in finding replacement employment. He cites two notably successful examples of workers being recycled. From 1982 to 1983, the workers at a soon-to-be-closed Ford Motor Company assembly plant in San Jose, California, were assisted by the retraining center run jointly by Ford and United Automobile Workers. Similarly, in 1985, the pharmaceutical company Ciba-Geigy, assisted by the Rhode Island Worker Resource Center (a state agency), made special efforts with regard to phasing out workers gradually, educating them for new jobs, and providing them with outplacement services when it closed down its Rhode Island plant. Now that legislation demands that notice of plant closings be given at least sixty days prior to their taking effect, companies will be expected to assume a responsible stance toward handling employees about to be laid off.

Alternative Work Options. One hallmark of the twenty-first century's emergent work climate will be alternative work options. Christensen (1989, pp. 3, 4), in a Conference Board report on a survey of over 500 firms, maintains: "As the twentieth century draws to a close, two types of work flexibility have emerged: flexible staffing, which has to do with hiring people on contingent and nonpermanent bases; and flexible scheduling, which pertains to how employees, once on the company payroll, are allowed to schedule their work days . . . the future of work force flexibility seems to rest in the area of flexible scheduling." Varied opportunities such as increased part-time work, job sharing, flextime, flexplace, and job redesign, all described in Chapter Four, will benefit not only the older worker but others too. Among these are middle-aged workers with responsibility for eldercare and women who do not wish to have to make a choice between being physically present with their children and maintaining continuity of employment.

Corporations, according to Peterson and Rosenblatt (1986), are beginning to address the need for alternative work options and nontraditional employee benefits. For example, The Travelers Corporation offers flextime, lunchtime support groups, and an information fair that affords employees who are themselves caregivers an opportunity to talk with social service professionals. Remington Products of Bridgeport, Connecticut, pays half the cost of parent sitters who provide respite for employees either on weekends or on nights during the week. Such practices by employers allow them to retain productive, experienced workers who might otherwise have had to resign. They also protect younger workers during slack time, as the part-time or seasonal workers will take time off then. At the same time, they enable the company to call upon a dependable, stable, and qualified labor pool during peak periods. The flexibility of such practices also serves to reinforce the loyalty of some retirees, who can now balance their work lives with leisure, volunteer work, education, or some combination of all three (Paul, 1987).

Top Management Commitment. It is essential that senior management subscribe to and support a continuing and viable role for older workers. It must be clearly stated and followed through by practices in:

- Organizational communications
- Managerial training
- Dissemination of accurate information to dispel myths about aging, especially those related to productivity and learning capacity
- Support for a wider range of employment alternatives
- Education about developing non-age-biased performance appraisal systems
- Education about reviewing the suitability of benefits packages for each age group
- Education about broadening of the concept of "reward" to quality of life issues
- Education about the advantages of educating older workers

In the Yankelovich survey mentioned in Chapter One (American Association of Retired Persons, 1985a), of 400 randomly selected companies having at least fifty employees, only one-third had received a formal commitment from top management to better utilize the skills of older workers. Failing this backing, there may be no widespread organizational support for equitable reassessment and modification of older-worker policies.

In order to develop effective managerial practices and HRD programs for older workers, one needs to understand not only how they are affected by organizational and environmental factors, but also what changes and challenges they face as they age. Chapter Three explores the human experience of growing old in America and its meaning for work life. As Nadler and Nadler (1989, p. 233) point out, "an employer who takes no interest in the nonwork life of an employee is naively ignoring those influences that impact upon the workplace, where people spend most of their waking hours!"

Chapter 3

Understanding
Older Workers:
The Human Factor

Aging is a leveling process. It is one of the few common denominators in America's graying youth culture. While personal wealth and health significantly affect how comfortably one grows old, we *all* experience the changes, opportunities, losses, and stereotyping associated with later maturity. In order to make better use of the older worker, managers must understand something about the personal meaning of aging and its social context. This human resource is a unique individual. How this person negotiates the aging process will, in part, determine the quality of his or her work life and performance.

The goal of this chapter is to contribute to managers' understanding of their older personnel as persons who work. If supervisors realize that there may be numerous factors operating when a fifty-year-old employee seems disinterested, or disinclined to work, they will be less likely to jump to the conclusion that such seeming lack of motivation is "natural" at that age. Nor will they automatically assume that the employee is "just coasting" until retirement. Since a corporate culture reflects the attitudes, norms, and values of the society at large, an organization's evaluation of and behavior toward older workers is colored by what society considers acceptable and accurate about growing old. This chapter, then, considers a number of human questions that have ramifications for the management of older workers.

What It Means to Be Old in America

As we saw in Chapter One, there is no universal agreement on what "old" means. The ADEA begins older-worker status at age forty. Bureau of Labor Statistics studies frequently begin it at age forty-five. Life-stage theorists often look to the fifties as the transition decade. Since sixty-five had been the traditional age for retirement and receipt of Social Security benefits, much of the literature on aging establishes this as the benchmark for becoming elderly. With the end of mandatory retirement, there is an increasing interest in the work of gerontologists, who now classify old age into *young old* (approximately sixty-five to seventy-five), *middle-old* (seventy-six to eighty-five), and *old-old* (over age eighty-five). Familiar, too, is the demographic reality that one of the fastest-growing population segments in the United States today is that of people over eighty-five years of age. No wonder the term *old* is problematic and relative. As stated earlier, age fifty demarcates an older worker in this book.

Evidence of the relativity of aging is part of the daily experience of each one of us. Comments like: "She certainly looks good for *her age,*" "Act your age!" or, "George, you're becoming a dirty old man," imply that there is only one definition of old age and that specific behaviors are appropriate to that stage in life. In actuality, persons age at different rates physically, mentally, and so on. Consequently, people who belong to a specific age cohort (the statistical term for an age group followed over time) become less alike as they grow old. For example, an enthusiastic and fun-loving co-worker of fifty-five may be mistaken for someone in his forties. On the other hand, a forty-eight-year-old whose skin has become wrinkled and whose hair has turned gray appears to be in his late fifties. Since it is thought that one's personality structure remains fairly constant throughout life, it is highly possible for workers in their sixties to be as peevish and insensitive, or as kind and flexible, as they were thirty years before.

One regularly hears stories of persons who make radical career shifts or start new families in their forties and fifties or

who uproot themselves geographically and socially in their sixties or seventies. It is clear that "growing old gracefully" has many
new and varied meanings for persons such as the fifty-six sep-
tuagenarians and octogenarians who ran the New York City
Marathon in 1987, or the eighty-nine-year-old student pilot and
ninety-one-year-old mountain climber mentioned in the same
Time article (Toufexis, 1988). Gerontologists no longer have to
point to singular artists and intellectuals such as Grandma Moses,
Albert Einstein, Pearl Buck, and Pablo Picasso to demonstrate
that creativity and intelligence can indeed blossom in an aging
body. Every man or woman can be exceptional in this way.

   Despite the litany of pro-elderly success stories in popular magazines, TV documentaries, and publications of organizations such as the AARP and the National Council on Aging
(NCOA), fear and denial of growing old permeate American
society. As Dangott and Kalish (1979, p. 13) comment, "old
usually refers to the way we see others." And indeed some of
these "others" may have Alzheimer's disease or another financially shattering and family-rending illness, or be institutionalized.

   While Americans over age fifty earn more than half the
nation's discretionary income (Toufexis, 1988), pockets of poverty do exist among the aging, especially women and minorities. *Truth About Aging* (American Association of Retired Persons,
1986c, p. 10) estimates: "Approximately 12 percent of persons
age fifty and above have incomes below the poverty line and
another 13 percent are considered 'near poor.' " Aging America
is not a monolith. It is more like a tapestry woven with fibers
of many colors and textures.

   Kenneth Dychtwald, a gerontologist and health promotion specialist, points out that prior to the current epoch in
American history, people did not grow old — they died (Toufexis,
1988). At the turn of the century, "old" was forty-seven years
of age. In contrast, a person who turned sixty-five in 1986 had
an average life expectancy of 16.9 more years. If one defines
"older adult" as a fifty-year-old, the significance of this segment
becomes even more pronounced: it is estimated that one in every
four Americans currently is over fifty and that by 2030 that ratio will be one in three.

   The lives of men and women who are now in their seventies or eighties have been a kaleidoscope of historical events. Far more than those in young or middle adulthood, they have experienced a holistic sense both of the life cycle and of the pageant of American history. As children, they were awed by such marvels as the invention of the automobile and the daring flight of the *Spirit of St. Louis,* which today's children consign to museums. For people who lost their hearing or experienced the death of loved ones in the influenza epidemic of 1918, it is awesome that infectious diseases until AIDS had practically been eliminated as major sources of mortality due to vast improvements in sanitation, public health, immunization, and antibiotics (Dychtwald, 1986). The country doctor who may have delivered some of these older adults using primitive instruments and who prescribed sulphur and molasses for their childhood illnesses is a dim memory. Elders for whom walking, horse and buggy, or trolleys were the major modes of transportation and letter writing the major mode of long-distance communication now observe or participate in satellite or computerized networks linking a worldwide global village.

Indeed, the lives of today's elderly have been personally touched by events that most adults have known only through the reading of history books. To persons who may have been educated as children in a one-room schoolhouse only during the months when the weather was unsuitable for farming, organ transplants, and spacecraft visiting the moon and Venus constitute a quantum leap in what can be believed or imagined. Women in this age cohort voted for the first time only in 1920. Everyone hoped that World War I would be the War to End All Wars. Then they watched that hope fade with the rise of totalitarian dictatorships in Germany, Italy, and Japan. These people came to adulthood in an economic system that valued the work ethic, long tenure with one company, loyalty to the employer, pride in one's work, productivity, and a nonparticipatory management system. Enduring and surviving the Great Depression made workers grateful for their employment and fostered frugality, hard work, and self-sacrifice. Age cohorts in their fifties and sixties have also lived through extensive and rapid advances but the range of their experience has not been as great.

Understanding How Older People Feel

Questioning the meaning of life, and confronting the reality that one will probably not attain all or even many of one's goals, are not usually the province of adults in their mid forties to mid fifties. Neither does mellowing and acceptance of past failures and accomplishments occur only in one's fifties. Such life reviews can take place any time, yet they occur more frequently and with more intensity with age. Stressing only, as some theories of human development do, the common elements in how people go through transitions, crises, stages, or events can provide an incomplete picture of their management. One must also consider individual variation. Upon the loss of a loved one, a person may grieve and experience certain stages that everyone goes through. However, each of us also lives through the process of grieving in our own way, showing a unique blend of characteristics as we express our personal feelings for the departed. Therefore, to understand what an older worker may be experiencing at a given time, we need to look at aging as both universal and individual.

Theories of adult development, if we select the relevant parts of them, can help us gain a psychological perspective on older persons as evolving personalities, balancing their personal beliefs and needs with the expectations placed on them by their employers and by society in general. Erikson, for example, postulates eight stages of ego development: (1) basic trust versus mistrust, (2) autonomy versus shame and doubt, (3) initiative versus guilt, (4) industry versus inferiority, (5) ego identity versus role confusion, (6) intimacy versus isolation, (7) generativity versus stagnation, and (8) integrity versus despair (Peterson, 1983). We will consider the last two as they encompass middle and late adulthood.

Stage seven (generativity versus stagnation) focuses on the pull between preoccupation with one's own or one's family's needs vis-à-vis devoting one's time and energy to addressing the needs of the larger society (generativity). For the worker who has begun to experience the leveling off of his or her career, it may be difficult to reach out and touch others through volunteer work or service on boards of community organizations. However, many adults do negotiate stage seven by making enough contributions to the next generation to progress into Erikson's stage eight. When people review their lives in stage eight and come to see the successes, omissions, joys, and sorrows as inevitable and acceptable, they may feel a sense of satisfaction (ego integrity). If, on the other hand, older adults feel regret, bitterness, anguish, and anger toward themselves and others over what might have been, they are likely to face their remaining years with a despairing attitude.

Vaillant (1977) has amended Erikson's model. The second of the stages added by him is relevant to this discussion as it takes place from about ages forty-five to fifty-five. The issues in this stage are ascertaining and maintaining meaning as opposed to becoming rigid in one's beliefs and behaviors. He depicts this as a stage in which adults begin to be concerned with finding meaning in their lives and struggle against falling into a rigid, fatalistic, and set orientation. Vaillant and other life-stage theorists cast the model of adult development similarly. They agree that there may be an early shift from concern with personal identity (Erikson's stage five) to concern with intimacy (Erikson's stage six); then to career consolidation (generativity); and, ultimately, to the search for and finding of meaning in one's life (Santrock, 1985).

These constructs, theoretical though they may be, attempt to place in a coherent and consistent framework real events and challenges happening to real people as they grow older. Havighurst (1973) has called these challenges the "developmental tasks" of middle and late adulthood, tasks that arise from the combined pressures of family, job, and community. These are, for instance, the tasks of defining one's roles in family relationships, such as to a spouse after the nest is emptied, to aging parents, and to teenage children in facilitating their growth to adulthood. Such tasks also involve the acceptance of civic and social responsibility and maintaining or modifying one's economic goals and standard of living in a more balanced life with increased leisure time.

Havighurst sees the final stage of maturity as a period more of preservation than of expansiveness. The tasks of later maturity include adaptation to the losses that happen over time, such as possible income reduction in retirement and the death of a spouse. These tasks refer to transformations in social roles. The loss of work, especially through retirement because of its connotation of finality, precipitates not only a 50 percent decline in income for a large segment of retirees (Peterson, 1983), but also the feeling that one has lost touch with a larger world. If one simultaneously experiences loss of the social role of worker, of a steady, decent income, and of a feeling of purpose, job loss can be emotionally debilitating. At the same time, if suitable replacements for the meaning that work held in one's life can be found by the worker, the effects of the transition can be greatly alleviated. For example, the former worker may find new and gratifying volunteer work or more creative and diverse leisure time pursuits.

Loss of the role of worker is not the only social role change people experience as they age. Death of a spouse, of siblings, of parents, and even of children can diminish the role of family member. It is up to the older adult to seek and secure outlets for creative intimacy in other family relationships such as grandparenting, to start a new family in later life regardless of societal norms, or to redefine "family" to include friends and then construct a family life built on this new definition. Common roles that one can take initiative in modifying are householder, citizen, learner, church member, consumer, and leisure time user. Other roles depend on one's world view, life-style, and how one feels most comfortable meeting the basic emotional needs of feeling wanted, worthwhile, secure, and competent, and above all, of being sufficiently independent so that one is not a burden to loved ones.

Another of Havighurst's tasks is to establish an explicit affiliation with one's age group. This as Cox (1984) affirms, is a particular challenge in American society, as many people refuse to accept the fact that they are growing old. In a Harris poll for the NCOA, only a small percentage of 4,250 interviewees regarded the years after sixty as the best ones of their lives (*The Myths and Realities of Aging*, 1979, p. 6).

According to Cox (1984), older adults make a conscious or unconscious choice to gradually disengage themselves from social and civic obligations while lessening their family and work responsibilities. They may opt to remain involved in activities associated with the life-style habits of middle age and replace lost opportunities with new ones suitable to their changing physique and shifting interests. They may continue roles consonant with their past history and preferred life-style. These are generally the roles seen by them as having paid off in terms of providing status and support.

Older people, according to Havighurst, also face the task of establishing satisfactory living arrangements. Basically, this means working out to one's satisfaction where and under what circumstances and with whom one will live in later life.

Finally, the aging person must accept and accommodate to declining strength and health. Despite the prevalence of the stereotype that old age is synonymous with poor health, and enough examples of cognitive, sensory, and general physiological deterioration to support the myth, over 75 percent of older adults are in good enough condition to maintain themselves and take part in their normal daily activities. With the exception of the onset of serious illness, aging takes place gradually enough for individuals to adapt and compensate.

Aging is, however, undeniably a progressively decremental process. One experiences loss of vision and hearing, as well as general inefficiency of the system. The immune system weakens over time so that it becomes more difficult to ward off illness. Decline of the nervous system can have effects such as shaking or confusion. Kidneys lose approximately 50 percent of their efficiency, making bladder control difficult. Lungs lose up to 50 percent of breathing capacity, which makes walking up stairs or other physical exertions more stressful than for a younger person (Toufexis, 1988).

The correlative feelings and behavioral responses of older adults to these physiological changes are as important as the changes themselves. The older person experiences aging in a variety of ways. One individual may become paranoid and withdraw from social interaction as his hearing deteriorates. Another may purchase a hearing aid, learn to read lips and to listen more attentively, and make any other needed adjustments with a minimum of anguish. One person may dwell on what he used to be able to accomplish quickly with better vision, while another will seek to harvest new memories by accepting the aging process, and by maximizing and building on his current skills and interests.

While the brain does lose about 20 percent of its weight and the speed of recall may slow, memory skills remain. The older adult who believes he or she is mentally deteriorating and identifies periodic lapses in memory as proof of mental decline can experience a steep drop in self-esteem and has, in effect, internalized the stereotype that all older persons develop serious memory problems. This is one reason why older workers do not request to take part in HRD programs: they may believe they are slow and not so sharp as they used to be, so why put themselves in a position where other people will notice?

It is important for managers of older workers to remember that there are great individual differences in aging. A fifty-year-old may be physically aged forty and aged thirty in terms of being a self-starter, ready to take on a new and challenging project. Supervisors need to learn to focus on what gains and retentions there are with aging, not on what has been lost. While physical changes and social role changes and tasks may prove imposing, individuals respond differently and, in part, according to their net resources — financial, health, psychological, and social. Older workers retain their learning capabilities, adaptability, and inclination to high productivity; they also benefit from their long history of creative coping in work and in life in general. As the corporate leaders quoted in Chapter One indicated, older workers tend to manifest steady work habits, are good examples of the work ethic for youth, are responsible, reliable, and satisfied, require less supervision once a task is mastered, and demonstrate minimal turnover, absenteeism, and tardiness. To be sure, not all of them have all these qualities to the same degree, just as all are not eqully successful in performing the developmental tasks of later maturity. But as a group they constitute too valuable a resource to ignore in favor of outmoded stereotypes.

The Costly Myths of Retirement

It is ironic that, given all the adaptations and accommodations they have had to make and the societal changes they have had to respond to, one of the major stereotypes of older adults is that they are set in their ways. *Webster's Ninth New Collegiate Dictionary* defines "stereotype" as a "standardized mental picture that is held in common by members of a group and that represents an oversimplified opinion, affective attitude, or uncritical judgment." Stereotyping is insidious and far-reaching in its consequences because it narrows thought and fosters self-fulfilling prophecies not only for the stereotypers but also for the group being stereotyped. Bridges (1977, p. 68) has observed: "Age stereotypes serve as self-fulfilling prophecies. To *expect* life to grow sad and thin after 60, and expect no new consuming interest after 50, is usually to be proven right."

The older male worker with a solid and proud work record who is three years from retirement may buy into the stereotype that he is over the hill and respond by ceasing to be productive. Or the still-handsome woman in her fifties, flooded with soap opera images of firm, trim, youthful females, may come to see in her mirror only the reflection of diminishing appeal.

While inaccurate, stereotypes such as those about older workers, discussed in Chapter One, impel younger persons and, too often, the elderly themselves to become fearful of growing old. They can even foster *ageism*, described by the psychiatrist Robert Butler (1973) as a kind of racism directed specifically against the old.

While retirement is not a focal point of this book, I offer it as an example of how age stereotypes operate in a work-related instance and of their subsequent effect on society, the older worker, and the corporation. The concept of retirement is itself stereotypical. For example, the word connotes "withdrawal," or "retreat" or "seclusion." One generally thinks of retiring *from* something, not retiring *to* a new and challenging activity.

Many older workers would not choose to retire. In 1985, over 35 percent of persons over age fifty, or 20 percent of the work force, were employed. Moreover, 10.8 percent of those over sixty-five, or 2.5 percent of the work force, remained employed (American Association of Retired Persons, 1987, pp. 11–12). In addition, a survey by the NCOA in the 1970s and a more recent study by the AARP revealed similar results, namely, that a fairly high percentage of older adults maintained their interest in working. The NCOA poll showed that about three-fourths of the elderly questioned wanted some kind of work, and 30 percent of the retired or unemployed older adults in the study specified that they wanted paid employment (*The Myths and Realities of Aging,* 1979).

Their preferences and behaviors stand in stark contrast to the stereotype that old-timers go to pick up that last formal paycheck recognizing that their productive years are gone and their accomplishments are memories. It is difficult for older employees not to subscribe to the myth of occupational decline over time as they are part of the larger society that accepts it. George Burns states in *How to Live to Be a Hundred* (1983, p. 131): "To me the biggest danger of retirement is what it can do to your attitude. When you have all that time on your hands, you think old, you act old."

For the society at large, as the baby boomers age, retirement will soon come to connote the heavy financial and psychic costs placed on those in young and middle adulthood. It could also mean the loss of vast reservoirs of maturity and talent if alternative work patterns do not become viable on a large scale. Corporations will find themselves competing for fewer young workers and will find a surfeit of employees in the age range of thirty-five to fifty-four. With people likely to find their careers plateauing earlier and with a scarcity of top management positions into which to move, more companies will most likely find themselves needing to experiment with alternative work arrangements. Among the options, as we have already seen, are job redesign, flextime, flexplace, and job sharing, which will accommodate the increasing diversity of the work force not only with regard to age, but also with regard to the needs of women and minorities who will make up over 80 percent of new entrants into the job market.

Companies will need to reorient their attitude to one of reinvestment in the older worker. Otherwise, they will run the risk that preretirees may act like bored short-timers as a quite rational and self-protective response to the predictable cessation of rewards and recognition and the attitude evinced by management that these workers are on their way out. The shock of the psychological impact of retirement even for someone who did his homework financially is manifest in this statement by Fitzgerald (1988, p. 102): "Most people think of work as what they do for a living, yet perhaps only in retirement they discover it is much of whom they have become."

The older worker cannot be viewed or treated solely as a performing member of an organization, as a participant in HRD programs, or as someone in the late stage of his or her career. Older workers are first and foremost *people*, who love, grow, fail, experience joy and loss, and accept or deny their own aging, defying or living out negative stereotypes of their behavior. And it is *people* whom managers direct, reward, educate, train, and develop. Leadership, motivation, delegation, and all the other dimensions of supervisory behavior depend on understanding how each person negotiates the numerous adjustments characteristic of later life described in this chapter.

Older workers have much to contribute, both before and after they retire *to* a second or third career, part-time or temporary work, full-time leisure or volunteerism. The next three chapters will describe programs and practices launched by some companies that have discovered this evolving fact of corporate life.

Chapter 4

Common Types of Human Resource Programs for Older Workers

Increasing numbers of older workers are resisting being shackled to early retirement by the golden handcuffs of benefit packages. They recognize, as do certain companies on the cutting edge of change, that an employee who must retool skills every seven to ten years anyway may as well be the mature fifty-year-old employee who will not turn over in three to four years. They deplore the loss of valuable and productive human resources like themselves. They see automation not as a displacer, but as a potential source of less strenuous jobs for those with physical problems and as an aid for those who need information in their work. Technology, it has been said, can either empower persons who specialize in *high tech* or support those in *high touch* — human service fields such as counseling and health care. Older workers resent being patronized, and they require meaningful work that fulfills a need — be it making meaningful social contacts, being helpful to other persons, or calling upon skills that they have already. Among these skills are innate analytical ability plus skills learned in school, such as reading and writing, or on the job, such as problem solving. Chapter Four discusses some typical human resource programs for older workers that respond to their need for fulfilling work.

The stated preference among older workers for both work itself and varied work options has led to the growth of a contingent work force — a labor pool totaling approximately 25 percent of the overall labor supply — comprising part-time, temporary, and fee-for-service contractors. An increasing number of contingent workers are older adults. This new segment, according to Lantos (1988), is seen as a mixed blessing in American society. It has been touted as the answer to both a company's seasonal swings in demand for workers and to the workers' need for a balance between work and leisure. Yet, at the same time, the specter looms of a predominantly female contingent work force exploited due to its lack of health and other benefits. Companies may also misuse contracting out because they can get the work done more cheaply than by hiring full-time workers. In so doing, they run the risk of reducing employee morale, heightening employee concern about job security, lowering quality standards if contract employees are not properly trained, and trading higher profits for the human factor (mentioned in Chapter Three). HRD, especially, can play an important role in educating managers about how to make maximum use of creative flexible work alternatives without exploiting the workers engaged in them. Learning programs on these options may be provided for company personnel, should top management decide some of these alternatives are feasible and appropriate.

Alternative Work Options

Less than one-third of the human resource professionals surveyed in the ASPA–Commerce Clearing House study supported flexible arrangements or shortened work schedules for older workers. Nevertheless, over one hundred companies serve as the vanguard for such efforts. The National Older Workers Information System (NOWIS), a computerized data base that originated in the early 1980s as a project of the Institute of Gerontology at the University of Michigan (it now functions under the auspices of the AARP), provides data on innovative corporate programs and practices related to the mature employee. NOWIS initially amassed information reflecting 369 work options; the results were published in *Managing a Changing Work Force* (American Association of Retired Persons, 1986a). An update, *Using the Experience of a Lifetime* (American Association of Retired Persons, 1988b), provides information on the practices of 100 companies. It is important to remember in considering this information that it is heavily weighted toward larger companies (73 percent had over 500 employees) and part-time work mainly in manufacturing and financial services. The study reflects essentially clerical and professional categories and places low emphasis on blue-collar employment. Another limitation is that it describes too many programs that are potentially tenuous or marginal in the sense that they will be the first to be dropped during downturns in the economy. Some of the opportunities it discusses tend to favor workers who have specific desirable technical skills or are in short supply (Root and Zarrugh, 1987).

In the preface to *Personnel Practices for an Aging Workforce: Private Sector Examples* (U.S. Senate, 1985), then-chairman of the Special Senate Committee on Aging, Senator John Heinz, commented that while the kinds of programs profiled in the NOWIS files are not common, they are "a basis upon which a major new approach to employment and retirement can be built." The programs that endure are the ones that mesh the growth and development needs of companies with those of employees. This section will treat definitions of various work alternatives and specific examples of how companies have implemented them.

HRD managers need to be knowledgeable not only about the specific kinds of options available, but also about what companies have used them, how they have implemented them, and what the participating companies' management has thought of their effectiveness. If the managers and their staff are familiar with such "packages" of older-worker programs and policies, they will be able to create informative and appropriate learning programs about them. Such programs should be made available to employees at all levels of the organization by the year 2000; not only could they enhance current and future job performance, but they could also serve as a means of promoting older-worker programs and policies internally. And they could make department managers more aware of what has worked for other companies, helping them to modify and customize the alternatives to fit the needs of their own organizations.

No one knows the full range and volume of alternative work arrangements for older workers. Quite independently of clearinghouses such as NOWIS, employers may provide part-time, temporary, or other options to employees, but information about them, which tends to be anecdotal, is not necessarily recorded in the formal literature. Some common alternative work options are described below (see Table 2). While numerous companies offer a variety of high-quality preretirement programs, I have not discussed them here. I believe that such programs, while providing some needed and valuable information on planning for the future, basically work against the concept of continued employment by older workers as they facilitate leaving rather than remaining in the work force. However, I have listed some books and articles on preretirement planning and programs in Resources for Further Information, at the end of the book.

Part-Time and Temporary Work. This primarily includes job adjustments made for retirees re-employed through job pools. Coberly (1985, p. 24) refers to a study conducted by the University of Southern California of part-time work arrangements in which "nearly half of the national sample of 2,382 employers indicated they rehired their employees." These new older-adult hires for part-time employment generally receive minimum-base wages and few or no fringe benefits. Some companies when rehiring their own employees will offer wages and benefits on a par with those earned by full-time employees. Root (1985, p. 14) states that "companies report that use of their own retirees significantly reduces the start-up time required by temporary replacements."

Table 2. Alternative Work Options.

1.	Part-time and temporary work
2.	Job redesign
3.	Older-worker training and education
4.	Next career preparation
5.	Wellness programming

The practice of using retiree job banks or pools, especially for clerical support, was one of the first of its kind. It is particularly common in financial service organizations such as banks and insurance companies, in some technical firms, and in fast food restaurants, all of which use their own or other companies' retirees for general short-term, full-time, and part-time assignments. Often preretirees are queried before leaving the company as to their interest in working after retirement and the nature of the work they would prefer; then they may become part of a computerized network that records their work schedule preferences, availability, and specific job skills. Companies such as Atlantic Richfield (ARCO) have taken action to modify their pension structures so as to accommodate their retirees. Sometimes pension plan stipulations have forced companies to contract out projects to retirees or work through outside agencies that act as employers of record. Generally, full retirement benefits continue when retirees return to work; however, eligibility for fringe benefits is not formally extended beyond what they would normally get in retirement. Moreover, wages and hours are monitored so that they do not place the worker at a disadvantage with regard to the Social Security earnings cap, or the employer at risk of the 1,000-hour rule (that is, beyond 1,000 hours of employment a year, employers must place the person on a pension plan) of the Employee Retirement Income Security Act (ERISA). Among the companies where annuitant pools have been used to mutual advantage are Lockheed Corporation, The Travelers Corporation, and Bankers Life and Casualty. Such employers have found that their job pools serve as a dependable supply of workers during peak season and enable them to extend service hours.

Reductions in the full-time work force of corporations have increased the need for short-time help. The phenomenon of organizational downsizing is likely to continue. In her interview with twenty-eight corporate executives, Axel (1989, pp. 14–15) found that several other factors besides the heavy demand for temporaries were driving the formation of job banks. Among these were that retirees were used to the company and therefore did not need orientation or, often, even training; they did not greatly increase overhead costs; and companies recognized they were losing some critical skills with early retirement when good workers left permanently. She cites (p. 15) John Young, chief executive of Hewlett-Packard, who stated a rationale for its developing its own flex force: "Because the company has a tradition of no layoffs, it was necessary to make it easy for a number of people to leave voluntarily. To avoid a similar situation in the future, the company is using more temporary and part-time people, a number of whom are retirees."

American Edwards Laboratories in Orange County, California, recruited older workers past retirement age to augment its health care equipment and supplies staff. It turned out to be a popular practice as managers' requests for such workers increased with the chance to observe their performance in such roles as laboratory aide or technician, word processor, maintenance engineer, bookkeeper, and clerical person (Humple and Lyons, 1983). In sales also, companies have found a niche for retired mature adults. Woodward and Lothrop retail stores in the Washington, D.C., area offered flexible hours for older workers. Other retailers, such as J. C. Penney, have encouraged their store managers to recruit and use retirees during the holiday season. The Aerospace Corporation, Los Angeles, has utilized an aging workforce well. In addition to providing pension accrual and other incentives for its older workers to remain with the company, Aerospace uses "casual employees," that is, retirees who work a reduced workweek adding up to no more than 1,000 hours a year while at the same time enjoying their retirement benefits (Paul, 1987).

Union Carbide Corporation permits hiring of its own retired workers on a part-time or temporary basis, without paying additional benefits, through an older-worker employment service that acts as a third party. The company has modified its pension plan to permit retirees to work up to 1,040 hours a year, thus facilitating their return to work. Texas Refinery of Fort Worth recruits retirees to join the sales force through a national advertising campaign. The company has found that persons over sixty are among the most productive staff. Naugles, Inc., a restaurant chain in the West, recruits older workers in the belief that they will have lower turnover costs, stabilize a young work force, and project a positive public image. F. W. Dodge Company, a national data-gathering firm based in Kansas, learned firsthand that their own retirees were more dependable than temporary help. They therefore redesigned some available jobs, which involved transferring data from completed building permits onto forms supplied by the company, into permanent part-time positions in such a way that retirees could work from three to four times a month or four to five times a week (National Alliance of Business, 1985; Axel, 1989).

The Sun Company in Radnor, Pennsylvania, experimented with hiring retirees for a variety of temporary positions including half-day executives, scientists, and production and clerical workers as early as 1979. Lazarus and Lauer (1985, p. 63), cite Robert Custer, director of retiree relations, who affirmed that "these people came in full of vigor, gave a full eight hours of work. . . . They were happy to be working again and wanted to do well so that they would be called back." Northrop Corporation uses an on-call work force of retirees with specialized skills that it can tap for special assignments on an as-needed basis. Grumman Corporation, which has never had a mandatory retirement policy, supports continued employment of its older personnel through its skill bank, among other practices. The company uses a number of its retirees for positions in engineering projects as machinists, inspectors, and so on, for its office on Long Island, New York.

Examples of corporations that have made use of older adults as full-time workers because of their acknowledged people skills are Western Savings and Loan in Arizona and Minnesota Title Financial Corporation. The former sought retirees for teller and hostess positions at the S & L's Westerner Clubs, open to customers who make large deposits; as many of the customers were themselves retired, they often felt more comfortable dealing with persons close in age to them. Employees age 65 and older receive fully paid health insurance and are entitled to participate in a profit-sharing plan and receive other benefits (American Association of Retired Persons, 1986a).

Hastings College of Law in San Francisco hired experienced *older* legal educators to teach in their programs. These instructors had had a wealth of life experience in both law and education, yet other schools had deemed them too old to work. Hastings's experience proved to be beneficial for both the school and the older workers (Dychtwald, 1989, p. 182).

Arkansas-based Wal-Mart, the discount store chain, provides second-career opportunities for older persons who may work at retail counters or in other roles that may lead to a management career. Approximately 7 percent of Wal-Mart's employees are aged fifty-five and over. Sam Walton, the company's founder and chairman, states: "Wal-Mart has found the older worker to be an experienced and dependable resource with strong moral and work ethics that have proven to be invaluable" ("Wal-Mart," 1988, p. 7).

Job sharing usually involves two part-time workers sharing one full-time job on a more or less permanent basis. It has been used effectively with older workers in both pre- and post-retirement. These persons may have individual accountability for getting their own part of the job done or they may share joint responsibility for the total job. This arrangement is implemented on a split-week schedule. The Wichita, Kansas Public School District, for example, has used this method for offering older teachers the chance to share their jobs with younger teachers until the older ones opt to retire. This setup provides the new teachers with mentors who, in turn, get the opportunity to gradually reduce their work hours. At the same time, it saves the school system the heavy costs of early retirement and the loss of older teachers' experience. Younger teachers are protected from the chance they might be laid off, while mature instructors are phased gradually into retirement (Coberly, 1985; Lazarus and Lauer, 1985).

Northern Natural Gas Company of Nebraska developed job-sharing options for retirees that provided them with reduced work schedules while they trained the younger, less-experienced workers with whom they shared jobs. Minnesota Title Financial Corporation has a successful and proven track record with job sharing, especially for the interoffice or foot messengers who pick up and deliver documents at law offices or banks in the Twin Cities metro area. Minnesota Title uses its own retirees as well as those of other companies to divide the messenger's job, usually by having two messengers work alternative months. There has been low turnover and the newly re-employed like the opportunity to make money, to exercise, and work in a low-stress capacity (U.S. Senate, 1985; American Association of Retired Persons, 1988b; "Companies Gear Up Programs . . . ," 1988).

Assistance to companies wishing to provide job-sharing arrangements is one of the numerous services provided by Operation ABLE. (ABLE stands for Ability Based on Long Experience.) Originally established in Chicago, this community-based effort has been duplicated in Boston and San Francisco, among other areas. Included in ABLE's activities to promote employment for persons over fifty are the operation of a job clearing-house to fill businesses' vacant positions, consultation on older-worker issues, and performance appraisal of older workers. In addition to providing a job club, job fairs, and a hotline for employment, ABLE also refers seniors to organizations that offer them training, placement, and job counseling (National Alliance of Business, 1985, p. 20). It also runs a service for persons seeking temporary employment in clerical positions.

Job Redesign. Companies use this approach less frequently than part-time or temporary work, as it is more costly in terms of the staff time needed to implement it. If job redesign were to be considered, HRD programs in a specific company would need to demonstrate if and how it could be done cost-effectively. Jobs may need to be modified in terms of physical environment, job responsibility, or scheduling. Control Data Corporation offers its employees flexplace, while it allows the disabled to work at home on assignments such as text editing through the use of advanced telecommunications. Such approaches can also benefit older employees and younger female workers with families.

Another type of job redesign involves (as sometimes does job sharing, too) rethinking and adjusting job responsibilities rather than technically modifying such physical aspects of the job as seating, lighting, or equipment. Job redesign is generally undertaken when older workers have had a long and fruitful association with a client, for example, in real estate or insurance. Sterile Design, a medical packaging firm in Florida, has rearranged its work schedule for assembly and packaging work to accommodate the needs of retirees in the Clearwater area. In order for workers not to exceed the Social Security limit on earnings, the company developed four-hour minishifts that allowed them to work up to twenty hours a week (Root, 1985; U.S. Senate, 1985).

Companies also make use of flextime arrangements that have great potential for older workers. Corning Glass Works of New York, for example, found flexible scheduling useful for its R & D division. At Control Data, employees have a voice in determining their own schedules, as long as they are available during the peak hours of 10 A.M. to 2 P.M. (American Association of Retired Persons, 1988b).

Sometimes rethinking a job and its match to a given employee involves providing for lateral or downward mobility. The Xerox Corporation provided a voluntary option for unionized hourly workers aged fifty-five and older with fifteen years of service or fifty years old with twenty years of service to bid downward for less stressful jobs at pay equal to the average salary for their former, higher-paying position. Such a salary adjustment would not affect a pension, since Xerox's pension plan is based on the last five years of service. A "down placement" option is also available at companies like Maremont, a producer of auto parts in Chicago (American Association of Retired Persons, 1986a, 1988b).

Older-Worker Training and Education. These programs are generally geared to workers aged forty-five to sixty who remain as full-time employees or to mature employees returning to the company after retirement. Training and education are used by companies when the cost of recruiting skilled personnel is expensive and time-consuming. An example is General Electric's shift to more sophisticated technology, a shift that involved educating the older engineers rather than laying them off. Generally such learning programs are used to help prevent skill obsolescence. Auto workers, for example, who have lost jobs due to plant closings and other adverse economic or technologically

induced conditions have undertaken training in welding and electronics. Mizock (1986) describes the nonprofit Senior Workers'
Action Program (SWAP) of Akron, Ohio, which educates older
adults in the use of computers and also acts as a placement service. Such services for education and employment challenge the
widespread ageist belief that older persons are reluctant to learn
new technologies or less adept at learning them.

Some firms have engaged in a kind of redundancy planning that keeps their workers from becoming outmoded and thus
"redundant"; this includes a commitment to employee education and training. AT&T and the Communications Workers
of America worked out a cooperative arrangement by which the
company agreed to provide learning for workers, many of them
older ones, who had been impacted by technological change.
McDonald's Corporation's McMasters Program, which will be
discussed in more depth in Chapter Six, offers a four-week education program with the aim of permanent placement for people
fifty years of age and older. General Motors (GM), as the result
of a contract with the United Auto Workers, set up a job pool
of laid-off workers to be educated for jobs within or outside GM
("Companies Gear Up Programs . . . ," 1988). Learning programs for older workers will be treated more fully in Chapter Six.

Next Career Preparation. The programs to be considered under
this head enable pre-retirement workers to retool for different
types of work either at their own company or, more commonly,
at another. Pitney-Bowes of Stamford, Connecticut, for example, provides a tuition reimbursement program for both employees and spouses over age fifty. Courses taken have included travel
agency work, secretarial skills, and photography. Companies
may include such a practice as part of their retirement preparation packages.

Some corporations have multifaceted rather than single-
focus career planning programs. IBM and Ford have developed
life-span career planning that includes such dimensions as multiple career paths, opportunities for on-the-job development,
career planning workshops, individual career counseling, and
mentor-protégé relationships. Lockheed supports New Career
Opportunities, Inc., a program headquartered in the state of

Washington that helps retirees upgrade and develop new skills they need to become successful entrepreneurs. Lockheed both contributes to the learning programs and provides funding to help the new businesses get off the ground. Levi Strauss provides financial support for education to its retirees and operates a program to involve them in the firm's community activities. Wells Fargo and Company offers a social service leave to employees who have worked three or more years for the organization; participants take a leave of up to six months for work in nonprofit agencies, engaging in activities such as fund-raising for an agency that serves developmentally disabled young adults (Root, 1985; Dychtwald, 1989). Career development for older workers will be discussed in more depth in Chapter Seven.

Wellness Programming. Despite reports by such companies as Travelers that the health expenses of younger workers have proven to be as great or greater than those of older ones, one of management's concerns about retraining older workers is the cost of health benefits. Maintaining and improving the health of employees of any age is a cost-effective means of providing greater continuity of employment, enhanced morale, and a possible decrease in health risks. Adolph Coors Company, for example, provides a cardiac fitness program for older employees. Evaluation of the program showed a decrease in time lost from work. Coberly (1985, p. 36) points out that "before this program was initiated, heart patients were off the job an average of seven and one-half months; the first 20 participants in the program averaged only a little over 2 months of missed work."

Companies such as Tenneco of Houston, Texas, offer health education seminars for older employees. Tenneco provides a four-hour class covering the topics of nutrition and aging, osteoporosis, and arthritis, plus an exercise demonstration: Aerobics Light and Walleyball, the latter being played according to the rules of volleyball on a racquetball court. Those employees who take part in the self-help program receive two books, *Growing Younger* and *Take Care of Yourself* (Levin, 1987).

More and more, as we have seen thus far in Chapter Four, organizations are placing value on the contributions of older workers. Orlando-based Walt Disney World Company places the approximately 9 percent of its work force that is older in varied positions, for example, in food service, maintenance, offices, parks, and amusement attractions. At Sea World, also in Orlando, mature employees make up at least 17 percent of the personnel during peak season. At O'Hare Field in Chicago, the nation's busiest airport, 25 percent of the employees of Andy Frain, a company in the crowd control business, are over age fifty-five. With its headquarters in Irvine, California, Builders Emporium, a retail building supplies chain, employs a work force statewide of which older workers comprise 12–15 percent; the company has observed that these workers relate well to customers (Match, 1987).

As Paul (1988) suggests, however, companies considering the use of varied work alternatives must consider certain factors in their own work climate:

1. *Programming of such alternatives must be compatible with the corporate culture.* Top management must believe that older-worker programs are consistent with "the way things are done around here."

2. *The programming must be consonant with the image that the corporation already possesses or desires to project.* For example, if a reputation for social responsibility is seen as desirable, flexible practices for older workers would serve the organization well.

3. *Older-worker programming must address an unmet need.* For example, if a given department believes it can enhance its productivity by holding on to valuable retiring employees, such programming should be adopted.

4. *The attitude of unions, where they operate, must be taken into consideration.* If part-time employment options are acceptable to a union, the program is much more likely to succeed.

5. *The prevailing business climate will be crucial.* The feasibility, success, and longevity of such programs depend to a great extent on how a company sees its prospects. During periods of necessary reductions in force (RIFs), companies are likely not to be philosophically or practically committed to such enterprises as coordinating a retiree job pool.

Federal Government Programs

Two significant federal programs that increase work opportunities for older persons are the Job Training Partnership Act (JTPA) of 1982 and the Senior Community Service Employment Program (SCSEP), established under Title V (1987) of the 1965 Older Americans Act. The intent of the JTPA was to train and place eligible unemployed persons in unsubsidized jobs. Features of this program that are particularly supportive of older persons are Title II-A and Title III.

Title II-A aims to improve the employment situation of the most economically at-risk groups, one of which is older workers. As much as 10 percent of the population served under Title II-A do not have to be financially disadvantaged, but they do have to have experienced other obstacles to being hired. Older workers fit into this category because of the prevalence of age discrimination. Section 124 of Title II-A, known as "the 3 percent program," sets aside this much funding specifically for training economically disadvantaged persons aged fifty-five and over. Most of the older persons served under the JTPA have come under this program.

Title III of the JTPA provides monies for training, placement, and other related assistance to dislocated workers. Again, a number of the persons who fit into this category are older adults. The issue of job dislocation is of great moment for older persons because once they lose a job, they are less likely than are younger persons to find employment soon and when they do are generally employed at a reduced income (Rupp, Bryant, Mantovani, and Rhoads, 1987, pp. 24–30).

JTPA programs have helped numerous older persons to secure jobs. According to the National Alliance of Business (1985), among the programs that have proven successful are:

- A Cleveland-based program, Skills Available, that has placed mature employees in private businesses
- A program in the Upper Cumberland District of Tennessee that has trained persons aged fifty and over for positions as aides and home companions to the aged

- The Intergenerational Day Care and Training Program of North Adams State College, in western Massachusetts, which has prepared older persons to be child-care workers

The second major federal program to be treated here is the SCSEP; set up under Title V of the Older Americans Act, it directly targets older people. Under this program, low-income persons who are aged fifty-five or older and who are capable of performing identified jobs become employed at minimum wage in a wide variety of part-time community service positions with either government agencies or not-for-profit organizations. Close to 100,000 older workers benefit from participation in the SCSEP each year. The NCOA is one of its national sponsors and, through its network of subgrantees, provides placement nationally for large numbers of mature workers (Rupp, Bryant, Mantovani, and Rhoads, 1987). The AARP is another organization that runs one of these programs.

Sandell (1988, p. 221) points out that state and local government initiatives, undertaken in conjunction with community groups and agencies, can supplement and support federal efforts to find work for older persons. Among the possible actions he deems feasible would be:

1. Modify civil service regulations so that permanent part-time work arrangements become possible.
2. Award seed money for creative programs that advance opportunities for older workers.
3. Formulate tax policies such as providing tax credits for organizations that hire older persons who are disadvantaged.

In Chapter Five, we will look more closely at some older-worker programs and practices. We will consider nine mini-case studies of companies that have put such programs into effect.

Chapter 5

Case Examples of Progressive Programs at Nine Corporations

While companies in general have been slow in responding to the new focus on older workers, some have taken a more active stance. Chapter Five presents vignettes of nine such organizations.

Paul (1983) has discussed the characteristics of twenty-five organizations that took the initiative in designing and executing programs and practices for older workers. Overall, she found that these companies tended to be employee-oriented: a basic belief of their corporate culture seemed to be that what benefited the employee ultimately benefited the organization. Therefore, they were sensitive to company morale, and perceived varied work alternatives as a "perk" that built good feelings. Second, the company managers who were interviewed described their corporations as forward-thinking. They had anticipated the demographic changes leading to an older work force and had planned in advance to manage their impact. They regarded work options as addressing the needs of growing numbers of middle-aged and older employees in a relatively inexpensive way. Another characteristic was that the managers who developed these programs were focused on reality and appeared not to deny their own aging. They reflected on their own career and work needs as they got older, and were therefore both creative in fashioning new programs and empathic toward their mature counterparts and subordinates.

Finally, Paul calls attention to the fact that the majority of the companies that assumed such a leadership role were non-unionized: of the twenty-five reviewed, only six had unions. In the latter cases, she points out, the unions supported such innovative programming and even, in two cases, proposed that the company undertake it.

Such vanguard companies are getting increasing and overdue recognition in the popular press and among older-worker organizations for their efforts. Dychtwald in *Age Wave* (1989) provides numerous examples of company initiatives to make work feasible and desirable for their mature employees. He maintains that emphasizing the *human* in human resource development pays off for both the worker and the company. He goes on (p. 175) to quote the Gray Panther leader Maggie Kuhn, who has contended that "the answer is in the workplace. If you humanize the workplace, restructure it around flextime, around mentoring, people will be less eager to retire. Personally, I want to die in an airport, briefcase in hand, mission accomplished." Companies like McDonald's, whose older-worker program will be described in further detail in Chapter Six, have derived immeasurable public relations benefits from their leadership in such programs in the fast food industry. At the same time, McDonald's has done much to rectify myths about the nonproductivity and passivity of older adults through its popular and much-praised "New Kid" and "Golden Moment" TV commercials, which portray its elder protagonists as competent and caring.

Whether retirees are working to augment inadequate incomes, to make a contribution to society, or simply to feel useful, they pull their weight. In fact, they behave like GRAMPIES, a term used by the marketing expert Sandra Van der Verve (Odiorne, 1988, p. 37) to mean "Growing number of people over sixty who are Retired, Active, Monied People In an Excellent State." Dychtwald points to the Naugles, Inc., chain that, after hiring older workers on a regular basis, found that its yearly turnover dropped from 400 percent to 80 percent. He also quotes Warren Buffet, chairman of Berkshire Hathaway and owner of several properties, including Furniture Mart. In describing the nonogenarian chairperson of the latter company,

Buffet (p. 180) remarked, "She is clearly gathering speed and may well reach her full potential in another 5-10 years."

The following are capsule portraits of some organizational programs that have demonstrated leadership in cultivating older-worker skills and talents. They are offered mainly as triggers to the creative thinking of departmental and of HRD managers for designing their own employment and learning programs.

Texas Refinery Corporation

Texas Refinery of Fort Worth has found retirees to be winners as salespeople of its building protectants and lubricants. Of the company's total sales force, foreign and domestic, of approximately three thousand, 500 are persons in their sixties, seventies or eighties. According to Jim Peel, a vice-president at TRC, this is not just humanitarianism: "We've prospered under the philosophy that you never put a man out to pasture. . . . I see older people who now have more energy than a lot of younger people. And they're more dedicated" (Bureau of National Affairs, 1987, p. 40). The majority of these employees function as part-time independent contractors who earn around $3,400 a year. The NOWIS Information Summary (*Texas Refinery Corporation,* 1987) cites company president Jerry Hopkins as regarding older workers as "more loyal and reliable" and as working harder than many younger employees.

Indeed, it was because of the management's firsthand experience of the "superior productivity" of older workers that the company adopted flexible policies regarding them. Among these is an age-neutral policy in hiring. The corporation looks at a prospective employee in terms of factors such as skill, motivation, and prior learning from life experience. New salespeople receive two days of intensive training and then begin work (U.S. Senate, 1985; American Association of Retired Persons, 1988b).

Kentucky Fried Chicken

The fast food industry has begun to feel the pressure of demographics. Younger workers are harder to come by and some of these are either not so dependable or so literate as an employer would like. So significant for the industry is this demographic challenge that Kentucky Fried Chicken (KFC) sponsored the first seminar on employing older workers, "Experience at Work," in July 1987, bringing together representatives from both the food service industry and older-worker service organizations ("Conference Explores . . . , 1987). KFC's response to this growing vacuum of capable young employees is their older-worker program, which they call "the Colonel's Tradition."

As *The Colonel's Tradition Brochure* (1988) affirms, such action truly does follow in its founder's footsteps: Colonel Harland D. Sanders began his franchise at age sixty-five. The Colonel's Tradition offers part-time and full-time jobs at all levels of the company. The kinds of jobs range from waiting on customers, preparing food, packaging orders, part-time management based on job sharing, or full-time management involving hiring, training, budgeting, and marketing. Placement depends on experience. According to KFC itself ("Press Release: The Colonel's Tradition," 1988), the company developed the position of part-time assistant manager to meet older-worker needs and to recruit older workers by its "competitive salaries and fringe benefits, including medical and life insurance and paid vacations and holidays." In addition to the attraction of varied activities—many workers are cross-trained in both customer and food services—and flexible hours, KFC offers a chance for promotion through its career advancement program, an oppportunity not generally provided even by some companies that value and maintain older-worker programs (*KFC Works for Older Workers,* n.d.).

The Travelers Corporation

In 1980, after a survey of retirees revealed that a number of them wanted to work, The Travelers Corporation of Hartford, Connecticut, launched its older Americans program. The program also answered the company's needs due to a shortage of persons with keyboard skills and the ease with which these "new" hires could be retrained. As early as 1970, this insurance and financial services firm was utilizing retirees in its consumer information area; sixteen employees shared four jobs. The position of coordinator of the company's job bank is itself a shared one. However, the 1980 study indicating that 85 percent of retirees wanted to return to work was the watershed in promoting greater opportunities for older workers.

The program did so well for both employees and company that The Travelers has extended it to include retirees from other firms, actively recruiting them through such strategies as job fairs and radio ads. The general procedure is that retirees register with the job bank for both set and flexible schedule positions in departments such as customer service, accounting, and bookkeeping. The company has even adjusted its pension plan to accommodate the needs of such personnel to work up to 960 hours per year without adversely impacting their health and pension income benefits.

In contrast to the myth about older workers being reluctant to engage in training, The Travelers found in a survey in the late 1980s that 65 percent of retirees queried who had at least typing skills had also expressed an interest in learning to use a computer. *Working Age* ("Corporate Ideas . . . ," 1988, p. 2) quoted Harold E. Johnson, senior vice-president for personnel and administration as saying that retirees were "willing and eager to use the latest technology"; the company's experience, he added, "certainly disproves the belief that older workers are incapable or unwilling to be retrained on computers."

In its aggressive "un-retirement" campaign to bring back retirees with data-processing experience and retrain them, The Travelers accelerated its computer training courses and paid the "unretired" workers during their training period. Handling the program in-house instead of hiring the workers through employment agencies has been cost-effective; The Travelers estimates that it saves approximately $1 million a year by employing retirees (U.S. Senate, 1985; American Association of Retired Persons, 1988b; "Corporate Ideas . . . ," 1988).

Boehringer Ingleheim Corporation

The low unemployment rate and relatively low numbers of job seekers aged eighteen to twenty-four in the Connecticut area where Boehringer Ingleheim operated was problematic for the pharmaceutical company until it started to tap the talent pool of older workers. The firm at first attempted to attract housewives by initiating a "mother's shift" that provided a flexible work schedule with abbreviated hours. Instead, the audience the recruiting campaign attracted was one of persons in their fifties, sixties, or older who stated a clear preference for part-year employment of four to six months, not part-time work.

Boehringer established a supplemental work force (SWF) that developed full-day and full-week schedules over several months. Over time this informal policy had "positive spill-over effects," according to William Kuchta, corporate director of compensation and benefits (1988, p. 2), in that some SWF members became full-time employees and some of the company's retirees joined the pool. Some of the older adults had not worked for a long time and could not adjust to the new work situation; others required a long time to train in the use of advanced pharmaceutical production machinery. But most did adapt.

How successful has the program become? Kuchta maintains that the SWF has worked so well that "we are now much more likely to hire a 55-year-old who may have elected early retirement from another company, or who may have been laid off as a result of downsizing (p. 2)." Moreover, the company is exploring "multi-directional career pathing" (MDCP), which would enable all employees to request a second career within Boeringer. They recognize that the staleness that mythmakers attribute to older workers is not inherent but a likely outcome of routinized work over a number of years.

Aerospace Corporation

Los Angeles–based Aerospace Corporation, a nonprofit, federally funded research and development center that provides technical support for national security programs, hires older workers both as full-time and as "casual" employees. It does so for positions at all levels of the company, in capacities such as engineer, scientist, and office, service, or shop worker. As far back as 1982, Robert Rubenstein (1982, p. 62), director of personnel operations, affirmed the significance of the company's "multi-faceted approach" that had permitted increasing numbers of older workers "to remain active contributors to company efforts." He went on to recommend that other companies use human resource development expertise and creativity to develop their own custom-tailored versions. In the mid 1970s, Aerospace began to bring its retirees back as needed in consultant roles that have been expanded due to the success of the program.

The company modified its pension plan to facilitate the use of its casual work force of retirees so that they can work up to 999 hours a year without negatively affecting pension benefits. Because Aerospace values both its long-term employees and continuity in work with clients, it has formed a retiree technical and administrative (job) pool and arranges assignments so that rehired persons often work with projects on which they consulted *before* they retired.

The Aerospace Corporation's use of older workers is testimony to their productivity. A Bureau of National Affairs special report (1987) cited Denise Jessup, Aerospace's retiree relations administrator, on the major role older employees play at Aerospace. She mentioned that in 1986 more than 40 percent of the company's work force was aged fifty or older, 15 percent aged sixty and over—the same percentage that was aged thirty and younger—and three to four percent aged sixty-five or older (Bureau of National Affairs, 1987; American Association of Retired Persons, 1988b; Axel, 1989).

Control Data Corporation

Headquartered in Minneapolis, the computer manufacturer and servicer Control Data Corporation provides a variety of opportunities for older workers. The home company operates Control Data Temps, a subsidiary that is a continuous source of permanent part-time workers; the firm has found that this arrangement saves both money and time in recruitment, orientation, and training. Part-time workers receive the same benefits as full-time employees with the exception of group health and life insurance. If a Control Data employee works 900 hours a year, he can be a member of the pension plan.

In order to ensure that its personnel are on the right career paths and to help them move into the appropriate positions within the company until they choose to retire, Control Data provides them with needed information. One example is a three-day course offered to professional employees between the ages of thirty and fifty-five; participants have a chance to assess their current career progression and make a lateral in-house transfer to a job more suited to their current goals and values.

Lifepath is a six-part preretirement planning program for employees and their spouses that enlists the participation of workers in plotting their own full-time future and beyond with the company. Among the multidimensional aspects of the program are a three-day workshop, support groups, and training relative to the older worker.

Control Data utilizes flextime and flexplace work options. A pioneer (since 1972) in the use of flextime, CD makes it possible for workers to set their own schedules provided they stay available for the peak business hours of 10 A.M. to 2 P.M. Its production line employees, who are interdependent in their activities, must come to agreement as a group on scheduling. The firm's flexplace system, called the alternative work site (AWS) program, though originally designed for disabled employees, is considered a viable full-time or part-time alternative for older workers. Such activities as text editing can easily be accomplished at home-based computer terminals (U.S. Senate, 1985; *Control Data,* 1987; Dychtwald, 1989).

Crouse-Hinds ECM

This manufacturer of electrical construction products, located in Syracuse, New York, has made a commitment to help its workers adjust to ongoing technological change. The Bureau of National Affairs' special report on older workers (1987, p. 98) quotes Julie Walter, manager of Crouse-Hinds as saying that the company "does not put our valued employees out on the street. We are retraining them and we're finding it's very successful." Interestingly, the firm is training its mature employees in the same kind of technology that other manufacturers believe they are too "backward" to learn, that is, computer assisted design (CAD) and computer assisted manufacturing (CAM). Management put its money where its mouth was and took the risk of investing $350,000 in training its workers, more than a third of whom were over age fifty.

In addition to providing for continuous skill retooling, Crouse-Hinds ECM offers cross-training — training workers in each department to do each others' jobs — to promote job security. The firm also encourages its preretirees to look toward part-time or second careers after leaving full-time work with it. For those retirees who want to work toward a degree or to engage in formal learning for sheer enjoyment, it provides a tuition assistance program. The company's dedication to ongoing professional development of its mature workers has won accolades from the U.S. Senate Special Committee on Aging and from *Modern Maturity* magazine (Bureau of National Affairs, 1987; *Crouse-Hinds ECM*, 1987).

Harris Trust and Savings Bank

Since the 1940s, Chicago's third-largest bank, Harris Trust and Savings, has employed its retirees part-time during peak periods. Impetus to accelerate and enlarge this practice occurred in the 1970s, according to its vice-president William Kottman (1988), head of its human resource staffing and development group, when the bank became Midwest correspondent for the stock transfer involving AT&T. While this event signaled a need to hire more people, they would be used only on a seasonal basis. The company therefore developed its Reserve Force, the purpose of which was to re-employ Harris retirees and other older workers on a temporary basis (Axel, 1989).

One particular advantage to older workers of joining the reserve is that they no longer have to volunteer to be available for at least six months; now they can work for as much as a few months at a time or as little as several days a month, as long as they agree to accept an assignment when it is given them. Members of the reserve work seasonally, during the tax season in the trust department, for example, or on an ongoing basis in such capacities as filing, accounting, and handling phone calls. Harris's experience with older workers challenges the stereotype that they are past the point of making a significant contribution to the organization. Kuchta comments about the members of the reserve: "In addition to the expertise they contribute, they act as effective teachers and role models for their younger counterparts" (Kottman, 1988, p. 4).

Cigna Corporation

Work-site wellness programs, while not older-worker employment programs, show that a company is willing to invest in its older employees and may make that company seem to be less of a risk to insurers in terms of health coverage, a major concern of prospective employers of older workers. If a company recognizes that over a quarter of a million days per year are lost to cardiovascular disease and hypertension (Dychtwald, 1986), and sees health promotion programs as decreasing that loss, it is less likely an older worker will be written off for hiring or retention. The Cigna Corporation of Philadelphia, an insurance company that also provides a broad range of financial services, initiated health education efforts that it then evaluated. According to *Working Age*, the company found that its "older participants experienced a reduction in risk factors for cardiovascular disease" ("Businesses Develop Wellness Programs . . . ," 1987, p. 3).

Cigna's preventive medical program, begun in 1979 for its executives to forestall heart disease and other conditions that may result from couch potato life-styles, was opened to all staff at the corporate headquarters. As Levin (1987) notes, Cigna is one of a small number of major employers that gives preference in the use of its wellness facility to older workers as a matter of equity, as they are much less likely to engage in team and individual sports. After an initial screening by medical department staff, the participants set goals in cooperation with an exercise physiologist. Then they engage in this custom-tailored exercise regimen. To encourage use of the facility, the company provides this opportunity free of charge and also picks up the tab for laundry services and clothing.

It is clear that the program pays off for employee and company alike. In 1985, Cigna chose as its first "participant of the month" at the Fitness Center its sixty-five-year-old vice-president. Levin states (p. 43): "Hypertensive and medicated upon entrance into the program, he has subsequently attained a normal blood pressure. A plaque on the wall of his office carries the motto 'Old Age and Treachery will Overcome Youth and Skill.' "

Chapter Six has a somewhat narrower focus than Chapter Five: it concentrates on learning programs for older workers. First, we will look at what some authorities consider to be appropriate styles of learning design and instruction for older workers. Next, we will look at some examples of actual learning programs.

Chapter 6

Setting Up
Effective Training,
Education, and
Development Programs

HRD managers who are considering whether to adopt or implement learning programs for older workers are naturally concerned about the relationship of age and productivity. This chapter offers both concepts and specific program suggestions for those managers who know and believe in older workers' performance capabilities.

There appears to have been a shift in the thinking of managers toward acknowledging the heterogeneity of mature employees and the inadequacy of chronological age as a measure of performance capacity. In a survey by William M. Mercer, Inc. (1981), 37 percent of the employers queried admitted they had some question about just how productive older workers could be. However, a Yankelovich survey for the AARP (American Association of Retired Persons, 1985a) produced results suggesting that one of the positive impressions managers held of older workers was that they were productive. Nevertheless, these same managers did perceive them as likely to be inflexible and hard to motivate (personal communication with Bernard Nash, director of AARP's Division of Business Partnership, July 1988). In her succinct summary of studies on job performance and age, Robinson (1983, p. 7) states: "The experiences of companies that never had an age limit for their work force or which hired older employees have been cited as evidence that older workers can perform as well or better than younger employees."

Replenishing the Mature Worker

As we saw in Chapter Three, sensitivity to the *human* aspect of human resource management and development is all-important at a time when everything is in flux. All workers, but in particular older ones, will require psychological support if an organiation is going to minimize resistance to change, compete, and thrive. Bracker and Pearson (1986) cite a survey of 322 human resource managers from *Fortune* 1,500 companies: three-quarters of them gauged that their employees were worried about or fearful of the rapid pace of technological advance (p. 110). Education and training can be costly, but it is no act of charity. Indeed, a survey of human resource managers conducted by The Washington Legal Foundation found that the number one human resource concern of employers was how to recruit and retain high-calibre employees ("Employers' Greatest Concern . . . ," 1989, p. 5).

Retaining seasoned employees has proven to be cost-effective for a company like Aetna Life and Casualty. Sherry Herschenroether, senior administrator for family services, reported in *The Aging Workforce* ("Improve Your Bottom Line . . . ," 1989, p. 3) that the studies she conducted for management showed that "it costs 93 percent of a person's salary to replace him or her — plus the 100 percent a company needs to pay the new recruit."

In the same article, Daniel Knowles, vice-president of human resource planning at Grumman Corporation, cited another apparent benefit in reinvesting in older workers: productivity. He recalled that his organization had found it necessary to lay off approximately thirteen thousand people between 1970 and 1977; the basis used for retention was performance, not seniority. After the layoffs ended, management found that "the average age of the workforce had gone up from 37 to 45 — suggesting a very strong, positive correlation between age and performance" (p. 3).

Rosen and Jerdee (1985b) have proposed an HRD program of the future for preventing employee obsolescence. Their method is to describe the HRD plan of a composite global high-tech firm that they call Multitech. Of particular relevance for older workers is the authors' vision of the five types of training programs, each for a special audience, that Multitech might create.

1. *Scientific and technical training, geared to engineers and scientists of any age*: This included a series of fifteen half-day programs to keep them current. Both in-house experts and visiting scholars served as instructors and were encouraged to provide a nonthreatening and friendly climate that would reduce the anxieties of senior scientists self-conscious about appearing outmoded to younger team members.

2. *Management development designed to foster the flexibility necessary to work in project management*: The firm mandates participation by its managers in at least forty hours of training on such topics as negotiation and problem solving. The firm develops its senior managers by supporting those who wish to attend university-based executive programs, by encouraging them to set personal goals for professional growth, and through a three-week course that engages them in the handling of simulated real-life problems.

3. *Training for production and administrative employees with a view to automating most procedures*: This is done on-site or through offers of tuition assistance and a training stipend to those workers who would be displaced. Since administrative staff are among the first to try out new technology, they are always up on the newest techniques and equipment.

4. *Corporate-wide programming that eliminates age barriers*: In addition to the traditional opportunities for skill updating, this program, through a training center, offers self-directed learning opportunities, internships, and job rotation, so that mentoring, coaching, temporary job assignments, and informal on-the-job learning take place for both senior and young employees.

5. *Retirement-related programs that consider preretirees' employment options in a practical light*: They include job banks that provide refresher courses for those whose skills are rusty and also support second careers through tuition reimbursement, at the home firm and elsewhere.

Learning Design

In a synthesis of key findings on the education and training of older adults, Sterns and Doverspike (1988) have reviewed five dimensions that need to be considered in developing such programs: motivation, structure, familiarity, organization, and time.

1. Motivation. Managers need to address such fears of older trainees as those of failure, embarassment, and inability to compete with younger co-workers. Supportiveness, encouragement, and positive feedback are therefore seen as essential to the cultivation of a motivating climate.

An environment conducive to confidence building, motivation, and commitment to learning may be the single major determinant of an HRD program's success, according to some sources discussed later in this chapter. Peterson (1983, p. 198) has suggested making learning more like a "game" to reduce the older participant's fears and anxieties. Rosen and Jerdee (1989) speak of the beneficial results that come from helping participants have faith in themselves and in their ability to accomplish the required tasks; they also stress the advisability of minimizing threatening elements. Belbin, as quoted by the Wisconsin Bureau on Aging (n.d., p. 6) believes that "the social and environmental situation that surrounds training seems to exercise a dominating influence on the results obtained." The National Council on the Aging National Work Group (1988), in its modules designed to prepare older adults to attain employment, continually emphasizes positive self-talk and self-appreciation; the council's system employs teams to discuss and to challenge the widespread myths and stereotypes discussed earlier in the book.

2. Structure. According to Sterns and Doverspike (1988, p. 101), the structure of a learning program should be such that "the material appears relevant, gives positive feedback, and encourages self-confidence for the trainee." It would also involve learning methods based on task accomplishment as the learner masters each facet of the task. As yet, in my opinion, there are no blueprints for learning programs that uniquely serve workers over age fifty; most programs are based on general principles of adult learning. What follows is an assemblage of ideas, prototheories, and seemingly relevant program structures that, based on my personal experience in educating laid-off older workers, I believe are applicable and useful. Among these are the same key elements of adult learning that, I have observed, still pertain as one grows older.

Mintz (1986) has suggested that facilitators of learning might use nonjudgmental small-group processes, especially for more difficult tasks, so that no older person would feel self-conscious. Such a structure could, in Mintz's estimation, reduce any fear of competition and establish upfront a collaborative framework for learning.

Peterson (1983) has suggested that Belbin's discovery method, used in the Aer Lingus study described later in this chapter, might be used effectively with mature workers. Though the strategy had not been used with any regularity with workers over age fifty-five, it is "based on insights from research on older persons" (p. 199). In the discovery method, learners solve problems for themselves and find out for themselves how something works. If they are to learn a new work process, the process is structured into a series of smaller tasks each of which is a unified whole. In this way, as they solve, with hints and cues provided, the problems associated with each step or task in the process, they feel a sense of accomplishment and mastery. Belbin (1970, p. 59) stresses that it is essential that all tasks not be "beyond the unaided accomplishment of the learner, even if he starts by knowing virtually nothing about a subject." Therefore, the role of the instructor revolves around introducing the problems or tasks, and acting as a consultant to and facilitator of learning.

Rosen and Jerdee (1989, p. 72) conclude that the most effective learning programs for older workers are those in which "traditional training techniques are calibrated to the learning styles of older workers." They lament the scarcity of research to date on mature workers' learning styles, but point to what they consider to be the most frequently made and effective modifications in HRD sessions for older workers or that include older workers. The techniques identified are: self-paced learning, training that has an experiential focus, coaching on the job, training that has direct and immediate application to the work situation, and learning design in which senior workers have provided input.

Gist, Rosen, and Schwoerer (1988) studied 146 adults, divided into two age categories of under forty and over forty, who took part in a three-hour education session in the use of a computer software program. They tested the relative efficacy of two teaching methods: (1) behavioral modeling by videotape followed by practice, and (2) interactive tutorial, providing immediate feedback that had to be attended to before the learner could continue. Results indicated that the modeling strategy was more effective for both groups. However, the older workers' comparatively low performance prompted review of the learning design in terms of the psychological factors that interacted with its structure. Among these were the timed aspect of the situation (three hours), which virtually eliminated self-pacing and, possibly, induced stress. Also, the actor in the behavioral modeling videotape was middle-aged and therefore not a relevant role model for workers over fifty. Still another consideration was that there was a cohort effect in lack of familiarity with computers; while all participants needed to have some knowledge of the technology, it is possible that the over-forty group overestimated their experience.

Advanced Automation Concepts, a computer research and training firm based in New York, conducted a study to identify "superior training techniques" for computer training "that can compensate for age-related needs" ("Research Findings . . . ," 1989, p. 5). One of the firm's findings was the importance for successful learning of organizing information for memory recall; they used, for example, visual images and analogies such as that of a file cabinet to help people remember the concept of a computer's memory bank. (The method is discussed in the last section of this chapter.) They found the discovery method of problem solving in an activity such as composing and editing a brief letter to work well for older participants, especially in combination with self-pacing. Program evaluators found one approach that was successful was the elimination of "strictly verbal step-by-step instruction." This observation supports Belbin's assertion (1970, p. 60) that verbal learning should be downplayed in educating older workers because of possible problems with short-term memory. Rather, the learning sessions were focused on two tasks, that is, generating a new document, and making modifications in existing text. According to Katka Hammond, coordinator of the study, "these defined tasks provided a context and a goal orientation to the learning process."

The sessions began with the trainer taking the lead by introducing students to the process and to appropriate terminology. After this, the instructor played a role similar to the "job coach" at McDonald's, that is, as demonstrator of techniques when needed, and helping hand in the practice parts of the sessions. All learning was supported by written materials such as brief handouts — again, similar to the McDonald's approach (see the section "McDonald's Corporation" later in this chapter).

3. Familiarity. Strategies that use familiarity with processes, tools, and equipment can enhance the self-confidence of older learners and underscore the applicability of what is being taught to their jobs. Lester (1985) observed that because of the importance of practical, job-centered learning to older workers, open-entry/open-exit learning done in the format of occupational clusters might be effective. In essence, a participant might enter or leave a program at any point once a desired skill had been mastered since the modules would be short-term and repeated periodically; for example, in an occupational cluster of modules on auto maintenance, the learner might opt just to attend the third module on brake servicing. The Wisconsin Bureau on Aging (n.d.) identifies such modular learning as one desirable structure for an effective training program; as the agency profiles it, "tiered training modules for older workers learning microcomputers might include: Simple data entry, word processing, computer operation and finally, computer programming" (p. 5).

4. Organization. The issue of organization concerns the observation in HRD situations that older adults tend not to organize new material in such a way that they easily remember it and recall it quickly when needed. The last part of this chapter deals with this matter in more depth.

5. Time. Finally, time is a factor that should be taken into consideration when educating or training older workers. Instructors should be aware that people learn at different rates and that some older adults — the population is too diverse to make a blanket generalization — may require self-pacing or slower presentation and study times (see also Goddard, 1987). Some studies, such as that by Ansley and Erber (1988), underscore the heterogeneity of older learners. In a comparative study that used a random sample of older adults and younger students, these authors found that there were no significant overall differences between the two groups in terms of pretreatment attitude toward computer interaction. In post-treatment, differences were consistent with prior attitude, in number of errors made, in the degree of cautiousness with which the tasks were approached and executed, and, interestingly, in the time needed by the older adults to carry out tasks.

A composite of instructional approaches for use with older workers follows in the next section. It is important to note that these same practices can be used with adult learners in general. In my opinion, what needs to be different is the primary focus of how they are implemented. Based on my personal experience as an instructor of older learners and also on the literature just reviewed, I have come to believe that the crucial elements of successful learning for them are (1) the context (environment) of the learning situation, that is, the degree of comfort, supportiveness, tolerance of mistakes, reduction of distractions and interference, and esteem building, and (2) learning designs that help them compensate for sensory, possible memory, and other kinds of decrements that come with age. As the Wisconsin Bureau on Aging (n.d., p. 3) states: "The way people learn changes over time. As certain skills or abilities decline, alternate ones develop or adjust to compensate." It was a finding of the aforementioned Advanced Automation Concepts study ("Research

Findings . . . ," 1989, p. 5) that appropriate and relevant learning programs in computer technology can, in the words of project coordinator Hammond, "definitely compensate for age-related deficits in memory or learning capacity."

The inventory below is one that I have used successfully with older adults; it is based on research mentioned in this and other chapters. For additional ideas, see *How to Train Older Workers* (Worker Equity Department, 1988b).

Instructional Approaches for Older Workers

1. Make clear to the older person what the purpose of the learning is and that it specifically relates to on-the-job tasks.
2. Consider the life and career stages of the learner and what this person finds rewarding at this point in time.
3. Be sensitive to fears about losing face and find mechanisms such as programmed instruction or small-group learning to offset them.
4. Relate all materials to skills and knowledge already attained and build on them wherever possible.
5. Actively involve them in the learning process so that it becomes meaningful, for example, through simulation games or exercises, computer-assisted instruction, case studies, critical incidents, problem solving, role-play, priority setting, or hands-on experience.
6. Recognize accomplishments in an appropriate fashion.
7. Whenever possible, use goal-setting and evaluation measures that have been decided on cooperatively.
8. Allow for the need some older learners may have for more time to practice and to learn new material.
9. Keep it simple by identifying a few key points and repeating them; where possible, model the desired behavior.
10. Use handouts and memory prompts, and organize the information to help learners retain and retrieve it.
11. Provide ample opportunity for questions, discussion, and mutual feedback about the content and the process.
12. Take into consideration sensory deficits when determining the physical environment, the design of the learning

experience, and the teaching method. For example, use nonglare blackboards, large print, and other easily perceived media, keeping a constant level of light and heat and speaking in a well-modulated voice. Take care, too, that the seating arrangements permit everyone to read an overhead transparency.

13. Create a friendly, relaxed, nonthreatening, noncompetitive atmosphere.

14. Where relevant, design an occupational cluster of skills (for example, skills for word processing could be broken down into five or six modules), so that participants can pick and choose appropriate modules based on their own knowledge and experience. The modules themselves could use task analysis as their framework. Learners would have a sense of accomplishment and, at several stages, task component, whole task, module, and job cluster.

15. When feasible, use older workers as peer trainers and facilitators. Taylor (1989, p. 48) states: "Be sure your teaching illustrations include mature individuals, and include them as positive models. . . . Invite older people as guest presenters or content experts, especially if your regular training staff is relatively young."

16. Where applicable, use the discovery learning method discussed earlier and, again, below.

The Aer Lingus Program

One of the most often-cited case studies, noteworthy because of its effectiveness in industrial training involving older workers up to age fifty-five, is that of Aer Lingus (Irish Airlines) in the early 1970s. The airline wanted to make the transition from a cargo warehouse with a shelves-and-forklifts technology to a semi-automated system based on electronically controlled storage and retrieval and a computerized documentation system. As described by Mullan and Gorman (1972), the training program had three phases. First came an orientation phase: workers and management met together in groups to discuss what changes needed to take place and why, and also how jobs would change. Throughout this part of the program, management reassured workers that they would retain their jobs, and that the "new" jobs would be designed to maximize the aspects of their jobs workers said they wanted to keep. During this period, those handling the change process endeavored to reduce anxiety and the reluctance to participate. The second phase of the program fostered ongoing dialogue between change designers and workers as to what the new system would and should be like. Finally, the actual training phase involved using the activity-discovery method of operating a machine and observing how it worked, followed by individual or group problem solving to correct glitches and quick feedback to alert operators to mistakes. Throughout this segment also, there was continuing communication between workers and representatives of management, who took suggestions for improvement from those who would actually be working with the equipment.

One of the reasons the Aer Lingus study became widely known in the field of industrial gerontology is that its outcome was that all older operators (those up to age fifty-five) achieved acceptable levels of job performance after the training program. Mullan and Gorman identified several dimensions of this training that produced successful results:

1. *Relevance:* Workers knew there would soon be change and that the training would help them adapt to it. Moreover, they learned through using simulated experiences or actual practice on machines; there was no abstract or extraneous material to digest.
2. *Self-pacing:* Learners could go more or less at their own pace.
3. *Involvement:* Workers were actively involved in the process all the way through, not only through hands-on learning, but also in terms of communicating their ideas to management and having them heeded where feasible.
4. *Anxiety reduction:* Management engaged in anxiety reduction techniques, such as providing support and encouragement, starting the training early enough for everyone to have a chance of mastering the needed skills, and eliminating formal testing in favor of simulations that indicated if a worker knew what he was doing. Older operators did ap-

pear worried about their ability to learn the redesigned jobs, but apparently ceased to be as they regularly experienced success.

5. *More breaks:* Older workers seemed to favor more frequent breaks as opposed to their younger counterparts, who practiced until they reached a "natural break" in the session (p. 36).

6. *Step-by-step learning:* The structure of the learning experience was such that each task started with basics and moved to increasing levels of complexity.

7. *Sensitive remedial help:* Management showed sensitivity to those older workers who manifested health or aptitude problems. They were offered the options of extra coaching on their own time or of repeating the session they found confusing. If they did so, it was under the guise that they were assisting the trainers in setting up the simulations and other exercises.

Mullan and Gorman (1972, p. 39) concluded that "if human aspects of change processes are ignored, it is small wonder that 'resistances' . . . are encountered. Both the planning and training methodologies utilized in this project . . . were particularly helpful in facilitating the adjustment of middle-aged and older workers."

Learning Programs in Practice

Some companies, as we have seen, offer at least some of the education and training described in Rosen and Jerdee's Multitech "blueprint." Grumman Corporation, for example, provides career development programs that appeal to mature workers; among these are mid-career training programs, sessions in management and professional development, and special programs for younger and older women employees. Included in the latter is the teaching of new skills through learning on the job (American Association of Retired Persons, 1988b).

The hospitality industry also has capitalized on workers' life experience. Management of the Days Inn in Atlanta has come to value the dependability, patience, and steadiness of its increasing number of older personnel. This third largest hotel chain in the United States has worked with the NCOA in setting up job fairs to recruit older employees for its 750 hotels across the country. *The Aging Workforce* ("Days Inns, NCOA Collaborate . . . ," 1988, p. 8) quotes Carol Bivens, Days Inns' vice-president for corporated communications as saying that "our corporate philosophy of hiring and training strongly affirms the value and capability of the older worker in society." Moreover, the Marriott Corporation and Aging in America (AIA) have cooperated in developing an education and employment program for older workers. According to Connelly (1987, p. 68), J. W. Marriott, chairman and CEO of the corporation, stated in his presentation at the annual stockholders' meeting: "We are looking not only for young workers but also older workers. If any of you want to come out of retirement and are willing to spend four hours or more a day working in . . . one of our hotels, we would be delighted to have you."

The Kentucky Fried Chicken franchise owned by Pete Harman, in conjunction with De Anza College in Cupertino, California, designed a twelve-week program in KFC's Colonel's Tradition program to equip older adults to assume jobs at all levels. Four weeks of classroom instruction prepared students for practical experience in the restaurants. The instructors were sensitive to problem areas such as seniors being concerned about learning to use the cash register; in such a case, the machine was brought into class and students had an opportunity to practice there before having to use it at the restaurant, thus reducing anxiety about manipulating the keys (*KFC Works for Older Workers,* n.d.).

The Travelers Corporation's management made an interesting discovery when it first re-employed retirees who had keyboard skills and educated them to use those skills for data processing. The company had designed peer training in small groups using hands-on practice. The students, however, did not want to be singled out for special treatment by age. They expressed a preference for learning in classes with employees in various age brackets (Hickey, 1988b). The design of The Travelers' computer literacy program had its origin in a survey of sample employees in home and field offices; it stresses relevant instruction in what an employee needs to know to get the job done. To achieve this aim, the program makes use of a variety of teaching modalities such as self-study, "student-tailored" instruction with diagnostic testing, interactive video with accompanying workbook, and computer-managed instruction. All include the option to pick and choose segments for self-pacing and pertinence to specific job tasks.

General Electric's Aerospace Electronic Systems, when faced in 1977 with the need to make a massive shift from analog to digital and large-scale integrated (lsi) technologies, designed the technical renewal program (TRP), which attracted as many of its engineers in the fifty-one to fifty-five age range as in the one from thirty-six to forty. The TRP, which reflected the company's overall commitment to learning for its employees, was a two-year, intensive training program, much of which was mandated and on company time. This program, as does much of the continuing engineering education program (CEEP), relied on more traditional class sessions, led by instructors. It did so because technology changes so fast that by the time media-based courses are developed to teach state-of-the-art technology, they are already outdated (Casner-Lotto, 1988; Hickey, 1988a).

Kelly Services of Troy, Michigan, endeavors to recruit older workers and retirees as they prefer and are well-suited for temporary or part-time projects. The firm offers "Kelly-Plus," an education program for those with rusty typing and shorthand skills, and also the Kelly PC-Pro(TM) System to enable members of its temporary force who have word-processing skills to learn a number of the major PC software packages (*Kelly Services, Inc.,* 1987).

McDonald's Corporation

Concerned, like other members of the fast food industry, about the decline in the number of young workers, McDonald's Pat Brophy, of the special employment division that handles the McJobs program for the disabled, predicted, "You're going to see a lot of silver hair in our stores and in our commercials"

("Companies Gear Up Programs . . . ," 1988, p. 1). Brophy also advised that businesses needed to be more creative in finding ways to utilize older workers, or they would be missing the boat for quality personnel.

As initiated in 1986, McDonald's McMasters Program provides skills education and placement in McDonald's restaurants for persons aged fifty-five and older. Under the terms of the program, McDonald's becomes a partner with a contracting government agency such as a state department for services to the aging, generally for a period of one year. Throughout the length of the contract, McDonald's employs and educates 80–100 workers of which approximately 70 percent stay to complete the learning sessions and work in its restaurants (some of the participants find that they are just not suited to work in the quick service industry). Both partners share the expense of the operation.

Job coaches are outstanding employees in the McDonald's chain who understand the values of the corporation well. They are selected to attend sessions at which they learn how to better manage older workers and how to both train them and facilitate their development (Stein, 1988). Once oriented and trained for four weeks by their job coaches, older workers assume various assignments in roles such as salad bar or drive-through attendant or as administrative assistant. The minor accommodations McDonald's may have to make — for instance, to provide a stool in the drive-through booth for older persons who cannot remain standing for a long time — is more than offset by the quality and efficiency of their performance. This statistic is particularly impressive when one considers that in the fast food industry the annual turnover rate for counter crews range from 100 to 300 percent (Bureau of National Affairs, 1987; "Companies Gear Up Programs . . . ," 1988).

While health, sick leave, and other benefits are not paid to these part-time workers, this does not seem to have been a concern of theirs, and they do have the opportunity for advancement. Older workers have graduated into such roles as job coach and management trainee on the swing shift, which is the bottom rung on the corporate management ladder ("McDonald's, with an Assist from NCOA . . . ," 1988, p. 8; *McMasters Brochure,* 1988).

An interview I had at McDonald's corporate headquarters in Oakbrook, Illinois, with Bill St. Clair, who is responsible for older-adult employment, highlighted the company's philosophy in this area. St. Clair commented that older-worker employment at McDonald's is nothing new; in 1972 at the restaurant where he first worked, "there were two employees in their seventies and five or six in their fifties." What is new is the concentrated effort to recruit persons over age fifty because of changing demographics. And the marketing — either through agencies on aging or direct company efforts — really works. Older adults are attracted to McDonald's because of the "family" atmosphere of the individual restaurant, or for reasons such as: "It makes me feel good about myself; it's the opportunity to meet people, to gain and share new experiences. The money's nice, but it's not primary."

As originally conceived, state agencies for older people (Maryland's, for example) would refer those they wished to place in jobs to McDonald's, which, in turn, conducted yearly classes of eight to ten or five to six people each at an estimated cost of $500–$700 per person. The agency would then reimburse McDonald's for the cost of the trainer and the company paid the employees while they attended the sessions.

Staff at McDonald's thoroughly screen potential participants in the educational sessions to make sure that there is a good fit between the person and the type of work. Since a number of these applicants have not worked in several years, the job coach concept was developed to facilitate transition to employment. According to St. Clair: "A full-time trainer–job coach could: (1) slide them into the job with a little more ease and comfort to allay any fears because they may not have been in the work force for a number of years; and (2) give them care and the personal attention they need to help them adjust, as all the buzzers, beepers, and timers going off all the time behind the counter can be very confusing." It is the job coach that is unique to the McMasters educational sessions.

The Learning Environment. St. Clair went on to say: "I don't think seniors learn any more slowly than anybody else. I think a lot of these stereotypes are just myths. We've had tremendous success. The secret is to just ease them in — to introduce them to one work station and make sure they feel comfortable there, then move them on to another." It is his opinion that the procedure is less important than making sure that people feel comfortable and enjoy the environment in which they learn and work.

Central to the McMasters Program is the premise that the company wants both its new and its seasoned employees to do well. St. Clair commented: "If you start from the assumption, as McDonald's does, that you want everyone to succeed, there is no reason why we should not be willing to take that extra step to ensure they are successful. It just takes support and confidence building — letting them know, 'Hey, we're going to help you and you'll be OK.' "

Learning Design and Methodology. Job coaches have the flexibility to adapt their approach to the group and to the customs of the geographic area. Martha Solgado, a job coach in the San Diego area, showed all her learners how to do all the jobs during the first week of education; during the second week she offered her students the opportunity to invite friends, spouses, and grandchildren to come to the restaurant to eat anything they cooked. This approach keeps things upbeat and makes learning and working fun.

The basic methodology, is as St. Clair sums it up, "See, show, do." This approach is used with all new recruits, not just older workers. All sessions are conducted on site at the particular restaurant where the potential employees are to work. Education makes heavy use of videotapes in which students observe an action describing the work station (in this case, for french fries) and then modeling the desired behaviors for that station. Each learner receives a station observation checklist, or SOC, which indicates, for example, the approximately thirty steps that need to be carried out at each station and relevant information about each step.

After participants have watched the videotape, the job coach will ask if anyone wants to try out what was demonstrated on it. If so, the job coach facilitates the process; if not, the coach repeats the appropriate behaviors seen on the tape. Then learners have a chance to practice the skills with the job coach monitoring performance. It is up to the job coach whether to move students through the stations in a group or individually; this assessment is based on their individual needs. The SOC is part of each employees' monthly performance review; supervisors use it not only to make suggested corrections, but also to "pump them up"—to tell them, "Say, you're doing a great job with us."

In St. Clair's view: "In 75 percent of the cases, older workers do not need to be trained differently from a forty-year-old or a twenty-year-old. Rather, we stress in our sensitivity/human relations session for managers working with older workers that, while people may have no noticeable physical limitations, you use your head—you use common sense and treat people appropriately. If people are sixty-five or seventy years old you're not going to ask them to bend over and pick up a couple of boxes of meat. Also, you ask people to do something; you never say 'Hey, YOU,' even under the pressure of the lunch rush." Although there is no conscious effort to do so yet, St. Clair would like to see the learning program modified so that there is peer education by older instructors. As the McDonald's videotape states, "Good people do good work, no matter what the age."

Organization for Remembering

The last section of this chapter deals with what Sterns and Doverspike (1988) have addressed in describing the organization aspect of a learning program. I consider assistance for remembering new material to be an often neglected yet significant aspect not only of "geragogy," that is, the "process involved in stimulating and helping elderly persons to learn" (John, 1988, p. 12), but also of any learning program.

Perlmutter (1988), in surveying the literature on adult cognition and learning, has reported that while there is some decline in some cognitive processes such as fluid intelligence— that is, the ability to make use of unique approaches to deal with unfamiliar problems—this is by no means universal or inevitable. Moreover, not only do most lifelong cognitive skills and abilities (for example, the ability to integrate information) improve with longevity but "some new cognitive abilities may emerge in later life, as long as adequate health is maintained" (p. 265).

Cognitive processes generally are described as including such facets as intelligence, logical thinking, memory, and creativity. While the interest in and motivation to learn new material may be detrimentally affected by behavioral slowing and psychosocial factors such as grieving over losses, dramatic decline in intellectual ability is not considered to take place in a health person until the eighties.

Memory is a cognitive process of particular significance in developing learning programs. My experience in designing such programs for both older adults and younger staff who work with them has convinced me that one of the underestimated reasons for older adults' seeming resistance to taking part in education or training is their fear that if they attempt to learn new material in public, they will demonstrate to others and to themselves that they are experiencing memory loss. For so many older people, this would signify the beginning of ultimate decline into senility. The effects of this stereotype can be debilitating, and the price of internalizing it is chronic frustration and diminished self-confidence.

Antidotes for the myth of inevitable mental deterioration with aging are greater dissemination of accurate information and learning programs designed to facilitate more efficient recall. Schulz (1988, p. 161) comments: "Information-processing research has confirmed that older adults perform more poorly on secondary memory tasks because they do not organize the material as effectively as do young adults." Some students of mnemonics encourage instruction of older adults in these techniques. In conducting memory enhancement classes for older persons I have found, however, that while they enjoy the exercises and it is reassuring to them to find that they are not on a greased slide into mental decline, in actuality they do not practice the techniques. An optional approach would be to include mnemonics in the actual design of the learning program.

There are various creative ways to assist older adults in organizing their learning for recall when needed. Harvey and Jahns (1988) suggest the use of *advance organizers,* which establish at the outset and throughout the education or training session a mental set for remembering. Among the examples they provide are:

1. *Outlining:* The teacher provides an outline of the module and of the day's class at the beginning, thereby setting up a logic of sequence and of relationship among concepts.
2. *Categories:* The teacher uses categories to logically and sensibly group several items under one heading. For example, if the discussion is about "wellness," the myriad of information that falls under this topic can be simplified into well-being of body, mind, spirit; then the categories can be further subdivided into subcategories. "Under body, one could group health care, exercise, nutrition, and so on" (p. 91). I have found this to be one of the most rewarding and useful mnemonics.
3. *Advance reminders:* At the start of the session, the teacher reviews key points, or questions which students need to be mindful of as they advance through the session.

All of the above strategies can be put into effect before instruction begins so that the instructor will be reinforcing concepts already familiar to participants.

Older persons tend to use external memory aids and feel comfortable with them. Therefore, instructors might want to make use of charts, handouts, lists, schedules set up in calendar form, and various types of recognition testing (such as multiple choice) rather than demands for free recall of new or long unused information (such as "On what date was the U.N. Charter signed?"). A valuable tool here for its repertoire of memory techniques is the NCOA's *A Memory Retention Course for the Aged* (Garfunkel and Landau, 1981).

Mnemonic techniques can also be incorporated in learning programs. The key to using mnemonics is to make the material simple, meaningful, and associated with material already known. Grade school teachers have long used rhyming rules (for example, "*i* before *e,* except after *c*") and created sentences to enable the class to retain the names of musical scales (**E**very **G**ood **B**oy **D**oes **F**ine) and other sequences. Visual imagery can also be utilized, but an instructor would need to take the students through a simulated experience rather than expecting them to do this independently, especially the first few times. A popular method using visualization is the location method. If an instructor wants a participant to remember five steps in word processing, she would invite trainees to visualize a place with which they are familiar, for example, their house or apartment, and then see themselves performing each of the five steps as they go through each room of the house. The instructor would thereby be using familiarity, visualization, and association (in this case, associating step with room) to facilitate memory. Another approach to encourage recall of the same five steps might be create a story — most students love anecdotes — that uses them. But because the story approach takes time and effort, it should be reserved for key or essential points.

An important aspect to consider about memory is that when a person says, "I forgot," it may be that he never "got" it at all. A person must pay attention to a fact, process, or piece of equipment sufficiently to notice it in the first place. If a trainee feels anxiety about training or retraining, it lessens his proclivity to "get" the information. Therefore, setting up a low-risk learning climate may help older persons in remembering.

Other factors about memory facilitation are that people tend to remember the first and last segments of a presentation better than the middle one; therefore, an instructor should introduce a presentation by listing key points and then repeat them at the end. A learning segment should start with a review of key points that the instructor desires to build on; repetition increases the likelihood of recall and diminishes the chances that the point repeated will be displaced by something new or forgotten over time. Moreover, a wide variety of teaching strategies, especially those directly involving the learner, with materials such as videos, case studies, actual work equipment, audiotapes, and so forth, will engage more than one of the learner's senses and enhance the possibility of recall.

Finally, there is the approach of positive self-programming for recall. Very often, as people grow older, they become anxious about their perceived increasing tendency to forget things. If they believe forgetfulness is an inevitable outcome of growing old for them, it can become a self-fulfilling prophecy. It is important, therefore, for instructors to encourage them to affirm their ability to retain and recall information when needed. For example, older workers, learning the WordPerfect computer software program may need to regularly and consistently assert to themselves, "I will remember that F8 is underline when I use this program."

Growing older should not preclude career growth. Chapter Seven looks at theories and programs that facilitate career development for older workers.

Chapter 7

Career Development
for Older Workers

Organizational career planning and development for older employees involves assessing both personal and corporate needs and then matching them as much as possible. This chapter considers career theory and then specific programs that have attempted to blend the organizational and the individual. Toward the latter part, I present my own career model for older persons.

Aspirations for opportunities on the career ladder must be consistent with the realities of available jobs and advancement within a given company. As Gutteridge and Hutcheson (1984, sec. 30.5) point out, career development (CD) in an organization consists of two distinct but related functions: career planning, which is performed by the individual, and career management, which is directed by the institution. With the evolution of a multicultural, older, and predominantly female work force, career planning takes on new meaning and new significance for HRD. While not strictly under the aegis of HRD, much of CD involves learning (Nadler and Nadler, 1989); consequently, the relationship of the two areas needs to be interactive, complementary, and symbiotic (Gutteridge and Hutcheson, 1984). Moreover, the growing trend toward reciprocal work contracts between employer and employee discussed in Chapter Two, as well as the prospect of an aging baby boom generation, reared on instant gratification, coming into later maturity at a time when employees' careers are likely to plateau earlier, compels new thinking about what constitutes career development.

Older workers offer unique challenges for HRD. As companies increasingly come to see the value of continuity of employment for mature workers, they must address those workers' concerns. In midlife, values may be in flux, and questioning of the place of work in one's worldview may begin or accelerate. People begin to frame their lives in terms of what they want to do in the time they have left and accept (or deny) the limits of their previously high expectations. Others may see this time of life as one of opportunity to pursue newly acquired interests through leisure or a second or third career, or to become one's own boss. Still others live in a state of chronic economic insecurity, anxious about the ever-present threat of technological displacement or of management subscribing to the myth of the outmoded older worker. Taking these issues into account, companies will need to create career directions for older employees that encompass yet transcend the alternative work options described earlier.

The Mature Employee and Career Change

Why do older persons seek second, third, or fourth careers? Bird (1988, p. 31) has summarized the results of a survey for *Modern Maturity* by affirming that, in addition to the need to generate more income, "this time around you want a job that adds zest to your life because it's fun to do, or takes you places you like to be, or puts new people into your life; or . . . there's something you know how to do that really needs doing." Some seek through new avenues the prestige and financial rewards that have eluded them thus far, while others welcome demotion or the assumption of entry-level work as a stress-reducer because it lessens responsibility and time pressures. For those whose special competencies are in demand, becoming a consultant holds appeal because it will enable them to choose their projects and how they will use their time. Career decisions are predicated on how one sees one's self and on what meaning work now holds in one's life.

As people mature, experience life's gains and losses, and pass through what have been labeled developmental stages, their life and career orientation alter. One's career, in particular, becomes a critical issue. Neugarten (1976), for example, indicates that while both men and women tend to become more reflective and introspective as they age, females begin to assert themselves more just as men come to place a higher value on relationships and on their own capacity for forming them. Thus, it is likely that both sexes will make career choices in middle to later adulthood that are quite different from the ones they made in their late twenties to early thirties. Awareness of the fluidity of personal growth can help organizations create harmony rather than conflict between their objectives and their employees' expectations.

Midcareer change is not necessarily a time of crisis; it can be a natural transition to an honest personal appraisal of one's current career path. The worker who cannot adjust his expectations of meteoric rise within his company to the fact that he has plateaued or who has internalized the stereotype that after age fifty, it's all downhill may experience reality shock after middle age. The worker who has accepted his level of progress within a firm may opt to continue along the same lines, putting more energy into his activities and assuming more responsibility; or he may decide to conserve energy by gradually detaching from commitment to the company. If an employee sees no hope for advancement and, at the same time, believes that it's too late to start over with another company, he can become fatalistic about the future of his work life and consequently demotivated.

Theories of Career Evolution

Career theorists acknowledge the role of socioemotional factors in career evolution. Schein (1971, 1978, 1985) has contributed concepts that need to be attended to in mapping career development for older workers. He characterizes career movement within one organization as being in three possible directions: vertical (that is, upward mobility), horizontal (that is, a lateral move), or radial. The last is often experienced by older executives as they find themselves being circulated farther and farther from the seat, secrets, and perks of power even while their influence still looks intact on the organization chart. He correlates career stages with specific tasks; for example, at the midcareer crisis stage (between ages thirty-five and forty-five), one may identify his *career anchor* and use it to conduct a realistic assessment of his work future. Schein's career anchor, according to Simonsen (1986, p. 72), is "that set of self-perceptions pertaining to your (1) motives and needs, (2) talents and skills, and (3) personal values that you would not give up if you were forced to make a choice." Examples of individuals' career anchors are autonomy, security, and service. If a person can identify at any point in her life what work is worth doing, she is likely to make accurate and relevant career decisions.

Heisler, Jones, and Benham (1988, p. 173) based on Schein's ideas about mobility in one company, described a *career progression cycle* for workers in general across organizations; it is modeled on the marketing concept of a product's life cycle. After a brief initial entry and orientation period, a worker moves into a growth phase in terms of both skill and responsibility and, possibly, into higher echelons of management. The maturity phase begins at different times for different employees depending on the individual and the corporation. It is a period of several years, the hallmarks of which are peak performance and high productivity occurring almost simultaneously with increasing limitations on opportunities for advancement. Many older workers are poised between this stage and the subsequent one of decline. The decline phase may be precipitated by such factors as skill obsolescence, burnout, or physical deterioration hindering one from adequately performing a job. Decline is likely, but not inevitable. There is, however, potential for a later renewal phase, depending on the attitude and actions of the worker and the organization.

As a constructive effort at recycling workers, Heisler, Jones, and Benham commends General Electric's Aerospace Electronic System's technical renewal program. They also maintain that companies can enhance the quality and viability of older employees' careers by devising strategies to prolong the maturity phase. The wisdom and practicality of this latter suggestion was acknowledged by Singleton (1983, p. 15) who called attention to the paradox that in American society, in which ageism is prevalent, corporations and governments often select persons over age fifty-five for leadership and decision-making roles. In attempting to answer why, Singleton identified skills that apparently improve with age, depending on the individual. Among these attributes were tolerance for alternate approaches and styles; ability to scan the big picture, quickly zeroing in on the essence of a problem; greater self-awareness concerning limitations and prejudices; and cooperativeness, with fewer competitive tendencies than youth.

Most career theories hold to the linear life plan, that is, that youth participates in education, while young adults work through late middle age, and the elderly engage in leisure activities. Such compartmentalization of life no longer fits an information-based society of aging baby boomers. Career planners of the future may need to consider a more cyclical approach, with people entering, exiting, and reentering the work force periodically and thus requiring constant education, training or retraining, and development. A middle-ager who is taking a learning sabbatical from his earlier chosen career or who has left the system for a time to refresh himself through a prolonged vacation may return interested in pursuing a completely new line of work. However, the individual does not make such a transition in isolation. Corporate reorganizations, mergers, acquisitions, layoffs, and technological change may impel an employee to rethink career direction.

A Yankelovich and Associates survey (1988, p. 36) of 3,000 middle-aged and older Americans, 1,000 of whom were sixty-five years of age and above, found that their subjects "would have continued to work if they could have." Work provides not only financial support, but also a link or "connectedness" with the society-at-large. One of the most effective techniques of coping with retirement, according to the interviewees, was in essence not to retire at all, but rather to continue working in the same position, on a flextime basis, or in a completely new career.

Corporate Career Development for Older Workers

Growing numbers of corporations and agencies are starting to afford their employees wider latitude in career management. Dychtwald (1989, p. 186) quotes Ed Shugrue of IBM on the company's career path opportunities: "We have assemblers who have become administrators, secretaries who have become programmers, and engineers who have become executives — not to mention executives who have become engineers." IBM provides the chance for employees not only to retrain regularly, but also to explore multiple career avenues within the system or across the life span. One vehicle for examining career options offered by IBM as well as by Pitney Bowes, Levi Strauss, and other corporations, is tuition reimbursement to retirees for taking courses in, for example, real estate, which could blossom into a second career or, at least, an additional source of income.

Pitney Bowes offers employees and their spouses over fifty years of age tuition reimbursement of $300 a year per person, up to a ceiling of $3,000. In this way, older workers can prepare for new careers (*Pitney Bowes, Inc.*, 1987). Stouffer Foods Corporation attempts to match employees' current levels of abilities with the tasks required by their jobs; for example, older workers who may have difficulty with a fast-paced production line can move to a slower one. The company also offers preretirement planning that covers the topic of starting a second career (*Stouffer Foods Corporation*, 1987). Control Data Corporation (CDC) recognizes that individuals change and, as they do, so may their job and career needs. To assist workers between the ages of thirty and fifty-five in such "midcareer correction," the firm provides a three-day course complete with a manual, *The Inventurers, Excursions in Life and Career Renewal*, designed cooperatively with the 3M Company. CDC sees this intervention as a means of helping current employees identify new careers within the company. Sometimes the new careers involve lateral moves that bring more personal and professional satisfaction than the old careers. (*Control Data*, 1987).

In the December 1988 issue of *The Aging Workforce* ("IBM Promotes Flexibility . . . ," 1988, p. 2), Mike Shore, a company spokesman for IBM, spoke of a program the company had under consideration to "increase productivity and loyalty . . . and to attract the best and brightest employees, young and old alike, and retain them." IBM's community service career program would encourage their retiring employees to explore second-career opportunities with not-for-profit agencies in the community; should these workers take full-time positions with such organizations, they will receive a portion of their company salaries as well as normal retirement benefits.

Not-for-profit agencies help older persons clarify career goals and direction. New Career Opportunities of Glendale, California, supported by grants and corporate contributions, conducts entrepreneurial training and offers free business counseling so that older persons can begin and successfully manage a home-based business — selling antiques, for example (*New Career Opportunities, Inc.,* 1987). Another such nonprofit organization headquartered in Los Angeles, it is financed by client companies' fees, placement fees paid by employers, and contributions from organizations and foundations. The program helps retirees locate jobs or volunteer opportunities, and works with client firms to design and set up preretirement programs that emphasize second careers and retiree relations ("Second Careers Program," 1987). The International Executive Service Corps of Stamford, Connecticut, works cooperatively with the United States government and over 200 American corporations in assigning older male and female executives overseas for two to three months at the request of foreign firms. The executives assist with problems in their areas of expertise, for example, banking systems, health care technology, and food production techniques (*International Executive Service Corps,* 1987). Maryland New Directions of Baltimore, Maryland, prepares women from early middle age to age sixty-five to enter for the first time or to reenter the job market through basic skills training and placement in internships tailored to their interests. Examples of placement sites are law offices and medical records departments in hospitals (*Maryland New Directions,* 1987). The Elder Craftsman, based in New York City, is a nonprofit organization that serves as a retail outlet for crafts manufactured by artisans between the ages of sixty and ninety. The Elder Craftsmen Training Studio provides workshops to teach craft skills to representatives of senior groups and senior centers (*The Elder Craftsmen,* 1987).

Partnerships for New Careers, financed by Hewlett-Packard, is a regionally coordinated retraining program that helps workers to move from progressively phased-out production jobs to clerical and computer positions. The three-month program, which blends academic and on-the-job experience, focuses on core skills training in such career areas as telemarketing operator, administrative support, and computer operator; participants learn or refine such skills as math, typing, and basic English. Ideally, the apprentice in a given job starts working at it simultaneously with the onset of training or as soon after that as possible. In each occupational field, management assigns the trainees a career mentor who oversees their schooling, provides encouragement, and acts as a linchpin relating content learned at the community college to job tasks (Casner-Lotto, 1988).

The Serial Career Experience

The meaning of "career" in America appears to be moving toward a definition that focuses mainly on a high degree of involvement (Lieberman and Lieberman, 1983). This definition appears to be displacing the multidimensional one that includes such facets as special preparation through education and training or increased financial remuneration. Studies of second and third careers in later life (for example, Clark, 1972) have described them as both hard to find and less meaningful than first careers. In their study of seventy persons in the age range of fifty to eighty-seven who engaged in selling arts and crafts at Florida fairs, Lieberman and Lieberman noted seven types of transition into second careers. These included midlife career changes entered into by professionals; displacement from prior work, for example, by skill obsolescence; self-chosen early retirement; actualization after retirement of goals conceived before it; search for a new identity by "empty nest" parents; continuing an earlier career in a new setting; and simultaneous practice of first and second careers.

Most if not all of these modes of change involve a need for income to a greater or less degree. Thus, the impetus for a second career may come from one or a mix of several forces. Those taking on the challenge of second, third, or later careers need to consider the degree of commitment they feel and are willing to make, and adjust their economic and professional goals to what is likely to happen. They must also realize that generally they will be beginning at entry level and therefore must start their careers all over again, perhaps by becoming apprentices.

The choice of a first career, compared with later ventures, involves a certain degree of leeway in exploration and testing to make sure the career line as experienced is compatible with one's goals and interests. Thus career development appears to go through at least five basic phases:

- Self-analysis of skills, interests, and values
- Occupational research to seek as suitable a fit as possible between oneself and one's career, including searching out specific firms one would like to work for in a desirable geographic area
- Filling in the gaps between the skills and abilities one has and those one must attain to perform well in the chosen career
- Marketing one's skills and abilities after estimating how the competition will present itself
- Decision making based on having identified, weighed, and perhaps tested out several alternatives

The last phase also would include a goal-setting component for one's advancement, with a feedback loop to periodic self-assessment (Bolles, 1988).

Older workers pursuing serial careers experience, in my opinion, a somewhat modified process. Based primarily on my work in assisting laid-off workers over age fifty in both looking for jobs and determining new career directions, I have developed a six-step serial career planning model (see Table 3). While the model could be used for young persons, it works best for older ones who bring a wealth of life experience to the decision-making process. The six steps are as follows.

Table 3. Six-Step Serial Career Planning Model.

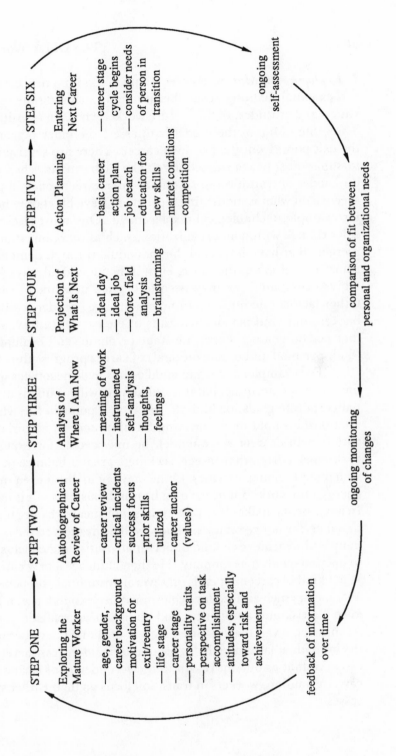

STEP ONE ⟶ STEP TWO ⟶ STEP THREE ⟶ STEP FOUR ⟶ STEP FIVE ⟶ STEP SIX

Exploring the Mature Worker

— age, gender, career background
— motivation for exit/reentry
— life stage
— career stage
— personality traits
— perspective on task accomplishment
— attitudes, especially toward risk and achievement

Autobiographical Review of Career

— career review
— critical incidents
— success focus
— prior skills utilized
— career anchor (values)

Analysis of Where I Am Now

— meaning of work
— instrumented self-analysis
— thoughts, feelings

Projection of What Is Next

— ideal day
— ideal job
— force field analysis
— brainstorming

Action Planning

— basic career action plan
— job search
— education for new skills
— market conditions
— competition

Entering Next Career

— career stage cycle begins
— consider needs of person in transition

ongoing self-assessment

comparison of fit between personal and organizational needs

ongoing monitoring of changes

feedback of information over time

1. Exploring the Mature Worker. In planning for a new career, it is essential that one probe the situation, including the motivation and attitudes, of the mature worker who is in transition. Thus, Step One in the model is to assess the older person at the exit point from the previous career. There are several factors that must be considered here. The Liebermans' schema of the modes of transition to second or later careers offers a perspective on what is motivating a person to leave his chosen field, for example, technological displacement. One must also consider change within an organization, such as reorganization or merger, that have impacted the individual through demotion, transfer, and so on; therefore, even if the individual stays with a given company, she may need to begin a new line of work. Other factors one must examine are the age, gender, cultural background, and personality traits of the person in flux, with that person's career stage, life stage or phase, and evaluation (both personal and organizational) of career progress thus far.

For example, as a white middle-class male negotiates midlife, he may determine that it is unlikely he will attain his original corporate goals for himself. He is at a point in life where relationships hold more meaning for him, and, in accordance with Schein's career stage model, he may decide for example to disengage from that career, seeking a greater balance in life with other fulfilling activities. Or he may opt to direct even more energy into work, but as his own boss in a business of his own. In any case, he makes his evaluation, supplemented by organizational performance reviews, of how well he has served the company and so achieves a kind of personally satisfying conclusion to his years with the company. He then launches a new career. What kind of career depends on several attitudinal and personality factors such as need for achievement, self-confidence, tolerance for risk and ambiguity, and ability to set realistic goals. At this step level, there is often a great deal of anxiety because the individual faces a high degree of uncertainty. It is therefore essential that as one moves on to the second step of reviewing career evolution, workers in transition focus on their earlier successes.

2. Autobiographical Review of Career. The second step, "where I come from," revolves around reflection on information in the worker's life history. I have used various approaches according to the profile of the group that is engaged in the learning experience. A common technique is for participants to sketch the progress of their careers in the form of a diagram, and to identify in that diagram, which often is simply a straight or erratic line, critical incidents in which they had to solve a problem or make an important decision that, in their estimation, turned out well. They can then focus on this successful milestone, indicating how they made their decision and why they feel it was a success. Thus, managers in transition or persons who aspire to management might look at how they executed well one of the common tasks of managers, for example, planning, organizing, communicating, and so on. If this were done in workshop format, participants would also, in looking at the same event, indicate what skills (for example, sales or mechanical) and abilities they activated, as well as what personal qualities (such as tact or patience) they demonstrated, giving specific examples.

It is useful at this step of career review to attempt to identify, through career milestones, what Schein calls the individual's career anchor. I have also used this approach with displacement homemakers attempting to reenter the job market and found that, by legitimizing and accepting homemaking as a career, they were able to easily identify skills transferable to the workplace. Such an autobiographical stance emphasizing successful incidents or transitions enhances self-esteem and enables workers to progress to Step Three. (It is important to understand, however, that insight into the appropriate career line and related decision making may occur at any step in the model.)

3. Analysis of Where I Am Now. In the third step, a mature worker must be willing to face some harsh realities and decide whether or not to make a commitment to a new career. At this point, the participants in a career planning program will need to take standardized personality, aptitude, and interest tests. At the same time, it is useful for them to reflect on their feelings and thoughts about using some of the skills they already have. It is not uncommon for people to be engaged in unfulfilling work because they have never taken the occasion to reflect that they have no interest in what they are doing. Workers in transition need to look especially at the interpersonal skills they bring to a job; these will be increasingly important in the multicultural workplace. I believe that the sine qua non of Step Three is for all to critically examine what meaning work holds for them at this particular time in their lives. If work is simply a way of maintaining a desired life-style, the nature of a new career may not be as important as its material benefits. If, however, one's work gives purpose to life, then it is crucial for both personal and professional growth that a new career fulfill that requirement.

4. Projection of What Is Next? For those who have made a tentative decision previously, Step Four should serve to consolidate or else to deflect them from that choice. Step Four concentrates on projecting what one really wants to do with his or her future work life and on framing this within realistic parameters. An approach that the author has used with some success in career workshops is to move people through their scenarios of a perfect workday to the construction of the ideal job; adjustment of expectations and hopes to reality comes through a subsequent force field analysis of what is workable, and through brainstorming on what resultant career avenues to take. The ideal day and the ideal job concepts are methods very commonly used in career programs such as those of Bolles (1988). Participants visualize completely independently, or through a guided fantasy, the kind of day in their work lives they would like to have, down to specifics such as how the offices look, the appearance of future co-workers, the exact job duties one performs, and so on.

In workshops they would share this vision and then progress from the micro to the macro view of this way of life as a career. In constructing the career they want, they need to look at personal factors such as what hours they want to work and what skills they intend to use, and at environmental factors such as what kind of an organization they are looking for (if not the one in which they are employed) — telecommunications, health care, and so on — as well as where geographically they want to do this. It is generally at this point that mature workers tend to notice gaps they need to fill in their skills, that is, they may wish to be involved in a specific line of work for which they are not qualified; education to fill in this skill vacuum may be necessary.

After Step Four, in which workers are encouraged to dream a little about a potential future, their vision must undergo reality testing through a force field analysis of forces supporting and restraining the desired change. In cases where various alternative career lines are possible, participants can conduct such an analysis on each one to assist them in making a final choice. If some career changers still cannot come to a decision at this point, a brainstorming session with peers may serve to creatively penetrate the barrier of confusion and generate alternative career directions. Ideally, most people would now be ready to move on to Step Five.

5. Action Planning. Action planning, which includes setting an overarching career goal, specific objectives, and timelines for accomplishment, would follow the traditional pattern followed in career workshops. For each objective, the planner needs to take into consideration problems she is likely to encounter, what resources she has or can generate, the support systems in place, self-selected and administered rewards, and techniques or tools of self-measurement of progress. Specific objectives may revolve around such facets of career planning as job search strategies and taking courses to learn new skills. In completing Step Five, participants will develop lists of problems and resources. For example, they can look at such factors as their marketability (already assessed in Step Three), what the current job market is like, who the competition is, and what they offer.

6. Entering the New Career. Usually, unless the new career has been an auxiliary one that is now assuming a primary role, people changing careers begin a new cycle of career stages and professional growth starting at entry level. Older workers have a vast reservoir of life experiences upon which to draw so that they can prevent mistakes committed in earlier careers from negatively affecting them this time around. As with the first step of exit from a prior career, the pivot is the *person* who is making the transition.

Entry into a second, third, or fourth career does not end the sequence. Actually, it is the *beginning* of information feedback on the ongoing interaction between individual, age, stage in career and life, appropriateness of the match between personal and organizational needs, and monitoring both satisfaction with goal attainment and changes in goals and values. This is the reason that Table 3 illustrates a loop effect in the model. When someone begins a second, third, or fourth career, he starts a new career cycle. Therefore, the model does not end with Step Six. Instead, Step Six, "Entering Next Career," leads to further assessment of self, personal and organizational needs, changes in the environment, and, finally, back to Step One and a retrospective look at one's personal and professional growth in the new career.

Facilitating career development is one dimension of a manager's role. Chapter Eight centers on management issues related to leading older workers. It also offers specific ideas for management training in older-worker issues.

Chapter 8

Managing Older Workers: Developing Needed Skills and Attitudes

A new work force requires a new kind of management. Chapter Eight takes up the specific knowledge bases, skills, and attitudes that managers need to acquire or cultivate to effectively supervise one group in this new work force — the older worker.

Because the information revolution and the pace of technological advance will necessitate constant retooling of skills, the manager of the future will need to be a facilitator of learning. At a time when higher levels of education will be needed and more sophisticated skills demanded, the labor pool will include greater numbers of immigrants and persons who have a literacy problem. Businesses will have to establish more partnerships and internships with educational institutions to make sure new entrants to the work force are qualified; they should also be prepared to fill in educational gaps at work.

The increasing cultural diversity of the work force calls for varied leadership styles and for rewards reflecting that diversity. The new work force will not be a melting pot; rather, it will consist of groups who assert their heritage, and call for its respect and recognition. Demonstrating increased sensitivity to appropriate treatment of women, minorities, and older workers will be a primary function of management. Supervisors will face the challenge of coordinating the efforts of people who work primarily at home computer terminals, of individuals who share full-time jobs, and of others who opt for the kinds of work alter-

101

natives described in earlier chapters. As corporations strive to compete and survive through flatter organizational structures and periodic trimming of labor-intensive operations, managers will find they must function more as coaches and as team leaders. Power will, most likely, be more dispersed as larger numbers of workers will have direct access to desired information through computer technology.

In deciding how best to manage any particular group or individual, a manager first should assess herself in terms of biases and ingrained stereotypes. This is especially important for the supervisor of older workers as ageism may be as entrenched in the American psyche as either racism or sexism. *Working Age* ("Understanding Older Workers," 1985, p. 4) has published a self-test that is useful for this purpose. When administered by the Conference Board of New York to executives of 363 companies, the test revealed that while they tended to view mature employees as loyal, productive, and dedicated, they expressed skepticism in the areas of motivation, flexibility, and adjustment to new technology. Such self-examination is valuable because it can pinpoint a perceptual problem that belongs to the administrator, not the employee. Faulty perceptions by managers can become visible in their behavior if, for example, they truly believe older subordinates have little capacity for growth and are likely to be resistant to computers, for then they will probably not recommend them for technological training.

Younger Manager, Older Worker

Younger managers who direct the activities of persons older than themselves may have to contend with the side effects of generational value differences. Recent MBAs entering an organization at the management level can face resentment from persons who have seniority and feel they know what is best for the organization. Long-term workers may also ask what right the younger manager has to direct and evaluate them when most of the manager's learning is from books, not on-line experience. If a young manager is laid back in manner, this may not sit well with older workers who have been taught the value of working long and hard. If they have been treated to controlling types of management, a participative style may, at first, make it seem as if the new boss is not willing to accept responsibility or assume a leadership role. A danger that young managers face in these situations is that they will avoid the issue out of fear of confrontation and thereby allow the problems to escalate. This understandable but regrettable reluctance to deal with performance or attitude issues in a straightforward fashion may only result in decreased respect, frustration on both ends, sloppy performance, demotivation and, possibly, outright hostility and subversion of authority.

Techniques for young managers to constructively and creatively deal with the performance problems of older workers may crystallize around the use of *management by objectives* (MBO) or other forms of mutual goal setting. Being allowed a part in setting their own objectives for achievement enhances employees' self-esteem and also suggests that management acknowledges their capabilities. Moreover, by placing the focus on the attainment or lack of accomplishment of goals identified by both parties, managers are under less pressure to criticize employees.

It is also desirable for young managers with limited supervisory experience to undergo management education that incorporates opportunities for learning techniques or problem solving and active listening. Generally, conscientious workers want feedback on their performance; what makes the difference is the manner and context within which the feedback is provided. Rosen and Jerdee (1985a) encourage managers to address the older worker's characteristic loyalty to the company by first identifying a performance problem and then stating it in terms of its adverse impact on the organization. For example, when a receptionist does not take the expected share of phone calls and messages, then others have to take on a greater volume and the company may incur costs in terms of having to hire additional support. If a manager presents a performance issue in non-judgmental terms as a problem that she will assist the mature employee in working through, asking questions such as "What do you need to perform this task?" and "How can I help you to get the job done?" it personalizes the matter and shows involvement and caring on her part. Such communication, which attends to the needs of the worker and puts the manager primarily in the role of listener and coach, demonstrates respect for the veteran worker's ability to contribute to solving the problem. Above all, it places both power and choice in the hands of the employee as he can decide if and how to improve. It also provides comfort to an older worker who now knows that he is not perceived as deadwood, and sees he has another chance, and can implement a chosen solution and periodically report on progress to a manager who is willing to listen and to help. Even when there is no problem with that person's work, a young manager needs to acknowledge the long and valuable work record of the subordinate in face-to-face meetings and ask for suggestions with the intention of putting the viable ones into effect. Psychological support by managers, coaches, or team leaders for employees will be increasingly important as corporations undergo rapid organizational change.

Bernard Nash, director of the division of business partnerships in the Worker Equity Division of the AARP, discussed in an interview with me what he believed to be key factors in managing older workers. Two of these are implied above, that is, setting up a facilitating climate for communication and for task accomplishment and also stroking the employee for work well done and for new skills acquired. It is essential that any compliments given be honest and sincere as patronizing accolades may be demeaning and cause the supervisor to be labelled a phony. Nash further admonished managers to get past the barriers imposed by societal stereotyping to genuine dialogue with older employees. In 1977, for example, Rosen and Jerdee had requested 1,570 subscribers to the *Harvard Business Review* (Rosen, 1978) to assume the role of an administrator who had to decide whether to approve a production employee's request for time and payment to attend a seminar; half of the executives had a simulated request from a young person and the other half from someone older. Results suggested the participants believed that the younger person wanted to keep her skills up to date while the older applicant was seen to be more concerned about getting her portion of the allotment for training. Since notably fewer of the executives approved training for the aging employee, it appeared that they were skeptical about the latter's motivation and capacity for learning and unwilling to make what they saw as a short-term investment in such a person. It is detrimental to such dialogue for a manager to automatically attribute a performance or seeming attitude problem to age. Finally, Nash recommended that managers focus on intergenerational issues and superordinate goals so that the emphasis is on working as a team to meet the team's goals. In that way, administrators can transcend value differences, including beliefs about the work ethic of age cohorts.

Motivating the Older Worker

Managers easily fall prey to the fallacy that older employees are hard to motivate. They fail to recognize that these employees are a diverse group with different needs. To prompt improvement in their performance, managers need to find the right "trigger" to pull. Nor do managers usually see any connection between the norms and values of the company's corporate culture and the older worker's disinterest or enthusiasm. If the culture of an organization values youth and newness and rapid change, it may unconsciously be sending the message that it does not value cumulative experience and loyalty. The disaffected older person may simply be logical and realistic in bowing to a fact of life in this particular system. Motivation moreover, may be based in part on perception. If the older individual perceives that the company will no longer promote him no matter how high the quality of his performance, or that the scarcity of feedback about his work may reflect management's belief that he is past his prime and not worth developing, he may become demotivated. Finally, managers may fail to see the role they play in causing the older worker to lose interest in productivity. It is easy to create a self-fulfilling prophecy: if a manager expects that an older person has peaked in performance and is just coasting until retirement, he will make no effort to recommend or provide educational opportunities for her. It is crucial that managers take a close look first at themselves, and then at the older worker in trying to decide if and why that worker has become demotivated.

In *How to Manage Older Workers,* the Worker Equity Department of the AARP (1988a) highlights their motivation, singling out financial security, social affiliation, and the desire to make a meaningful contribution as primary needs for the majority. Others have pointed to additional needs such as recognition, alleviation of dependency, and the desire to remain functional and active.

Engaging in mutual goal setting with management reduces older workers' anxiety, according to the AARP publication, because the workers have input and can tell exactly what is expected when. Such an arrangement shows respect for their ideas and also promotes the feeling that they have some control over their own futures. The work objectives, whether defined in terms of market share, products, sales, or something else, are accepted as feasible and measurable. Both they and the time frames are seen not as assignments imposed from the top down, but rather as resulting from a negotiation to which each person has made a contribution. However, MBO or some other cooperative goal-setting technique will be effective only if the goals are truly attainable, employees are given the needed resoures to accomplish their tasks, evaluation focuses on what went excellently as well as badly, and their rewards are meaningful, suitable, and address the needs mentioned earlier.

Managers may acknowledge an older worker's attainments by consulting with her on new or related projects, involving her in problem solving connected to her line of work, publicizing her achievement on a companywide level and, possibly, through adjusting her job title or responsibilities. Involving the older worker in task forces, decision-making sessions, and project teams communicates to all employees the value top management places on experience.

Job redesign, cross-training, and other job modifications can keep older workers motivated because such efforts reduce the boredom inherent in narrow, routine work done over time. Above all, a manager's willingness to spend time with an older worker, whether lauding or encouraging his efforts, providing constructive feedback on how he's doing, or soliciting input before initiating program or policy changes, can be a major force in keeping him motivated. Keeping the channels of communication open is paramount. In talking with older workers, managers may find a shift in focus—a concern for quality of life, a desire to live a broader, more meaningful life in which work assumes a lesser role. This does not necessarily mean the worker has become impossible to motivate. Rather, the manager faces the challenge of determining the nature of the need shift and matching it with appropriate rewards.

Plateaued employees are often ones who have practiced their one area of expertise in the same job for several years. Many of these are older. Usually, they are perceived as, and indeed may actually be, devitalized and discouraged, having come to feel they have no control over their corporate fate.

Organizations can take more initiative in assisting workers who appear to have leveled off with regard to corporate advancement and who may no longer seem to be keeping their skills up to par. Strategies that companies need to consider include some of the alternative work options mentioned in Chapter Four: for example, training, job redesign, and job transfer, as well as mentoring, coaching, and involving these employees in teams to raise the quality of work life.

A manager who is sensitive to the kinds of psychosocial changes, described in Chapter Three, that an older person may be experiencing, may be of great help to the plateaued employee by listening and showing concern. Giving the employee a chance to say how existing skills could be put to better use and what new skills could lead to more challenging work, even in a lateral transfer, may reduce that employee's anxiety and stress. Bardwick (1986) has mentioned how helpful it can be if the manager simply gets in the habit of walking around. According to her view of the manager and the plateaued employee, "managers who have continuous, informal, spontaneous exchanges with those who work for them are creating the opportunity for honesty, for counseling, for the reassurance that you know employees exist and that they care" (p. 161).

Additional ways of preventing plateauing among older workers have been suggested by Suzanne Minken, president of The Minken Group in New York City, who believes in innovative approaches to compensation ("New Strategies Can Motivate . . . ," 1989, pp. 134-135). Among these are:

- *Key contributor incentives,* with the number of incentive units based on length of service
- *Skill-based pay,* with the specific intent of motivating workers to increase their skill base
- *Lump sum merit pay,* with merit increase awarded on the anniversary date
- *Supplemental performance awards,* with opportunities to win available across the board regardless of age

Stress and the Older Worker

Closely related to the issue of motivation and demotivation is the impact of stress on the older worker. One tenet of the holistic health movement is that stress can be beneficial up to a point that varies from person to person; *eustress,* that is, positive stress, while chronic or other types of unmanaged stress can act as demotivators. Older adults in particular are at risk for being sandwiched between sources of stress at work and in the home. For example, a fifty-year-old may face the pressures of eldercare at home as well as competition with younger workers on the job; indeed, stress experienced from diverse sources can be additive. Since older workers may be experiencing several losses simultaneously — for example, death or relocation of friends and family members — coping with stress in the workplace may be more difficult than for younger employees.

Causes of workplace stress for older workers are varied and must be understood and sensitively handled by managers. Dealing with myths about aging, such as that all older persons are resistant to change, is stressful — especially when one knows that adaptation to change is a highly individual matter. Many years in a mind-blurring, repetitious job may induce burnout. An older worker may be facing two limited futures, one with the company and one in terms of mortality. Lack of feedback on performance can create stress because people like to know where they stand even if they are catching errors; also a superior who talks less frequently with an older employee than with a younger peer may give the impression that he values the older one's work less. Women who are returning to the work force after many years are especially prone to stress from uncertainty about self-worth and personal competence as they update old skills and endeavor to acquire new ones. An older employee may experience stress as he interacts regularly with young counterparts who know he will not be advancing up the corporate ladder with them or who believe he will soon be put out to pasture. He may also suspect that in an economic pinch his job would be among the first to be eliminated.

HRD managers, as well as managers of departments, can take the initiative in helping to alleviate some sources of stress for older employees by providing appropriate management education. Managers should learn to be aware of and sensitive to differences among people and to the changes an individual undergoes with age, so that they will recognize when an older employee appears stressed. Recent irritability, incipient cynicism, drops in productivity, increase in mistakes, depressiveness, withdrawal, or seeming chronic fatigue may all be trouble signals. The manager should seek an opportunity to open communication with an expression of care and concern, for example, "It seems to me that you've been very tired every day for a while now, and I've become concerned that something's wrong." Should the older worker shrug it off, the manager will at least have expressed interest and laid the groundwork for a possible future encounter of trust. Should the older person open up at this point, the manager should be prepared to sit down and listen attentively and talk about the matter. If the problem concerns something over which the manager has control, such as job structure, immediate action may be taken in terms of job redesign. If the issue is fear of layoff, the manager may be able to reduce it, but no promise should be made that cannot be kept. Problems with personal matters such as caring for an elderly parent may be handled through appropriate referrals. Managers can learn about referral sources in their management training.

Their jobs play a major role in the lives of today's older workers. They are proud of the work they do and much of their self-esteem is connected with it. If and when a manager can help lift the burden of stress from these capable people, they will have the freedom to show how productive they can be.

Management Training

Many of the trends reviewed earlier suggest that managers in the future will have to supervise greater numbers of older workers. The rate at which new jobs are being created is outstripping the growth rate of the labor force; there is growing concern about the financial and psychic costs of early retirement for society and for individual corporations; and an emerging body of data indicates the significant portion of older workers who wish to continue in that social role would be an asset to their organizations. One of the major challenges to human resource development in the 1990s is therefore two-pronged: The need to establish appropriate learning programs for workers, and the related need to train managers in step with the new definition of what the term *manage* means.

Kravetz (1988) describes the shift from the close supervision of workers of the industrial period to the facilitation of a team performing on a flexible schedule from far-flung home bases in the new information society. Today's manager, to get the job done, may operate in a flatter, less hierarchical structure and need to exercise leadership over people from various areas of the organization. Therefore, skill development in project management, effective communication, team building, and problem solving are all essential for directing the efforts of people of all ages. Managers will need to assess employees in terms of the quality and quantity of assignments or projects they have accomplished rather than how much time they have put in; this will be especially important given the increase in work options such as flexible scheduling and job sharing. Since workers will be able to access the information they need directly through desk computer terminals, for example, the manager will not serve the role of primary information disseminator; if information is power, power will be more diffused. The manager of the 1990s will be a symphony orchestra conductor of sorts, making sure the group functions in harmony, being so sensitive to the functioning of individuals that she can hear dissonance, recognizing and respecting the uniqueness of each instrument and player, and trusting them with the responsibility and authority to perform their parts with such creativity that they create synergy for the orchestra.

Because the workplace is becoming more feminine, multicultural, and multigenerational, managers must also have a greater understanding of the value and contributions of diversity. It is essential for the flowering of authentic participative mangement in a given company that managers grow in awareness of the nature of the various segments in their work force. One of these segments is older workers.

Research centers such as the Andrus Gerontology Center at the University of Southern California (Dennis and Peterson, 1983), as well as organizations such as the American Management Association (Humple and Lyons, 1983), have published reports or manuals on training management about older employees. What follows is a composite (see Table 4) of the content of several such programs. An introductory session would explain the reasons for learning this material: the changing demographics, the changing economic focus (including the growing financial burden of early retirement), and the changing personnel and technological profile of the company itself.

1. Self-Assessment by Managers. Prior to any attempts by supervisors of older workers to correct faulty perceptions of older

Table 4. Composite of Corporate Management
Training Programs Related to Older Workers.

1.	Self-assessment by managers
2.	Myths and stereotypes of growing old
3.	Life development and changes
4.	Dynamics of workplace interaction
5.	Action planning

workers' capabilities, it is important for supervisors to consider their own attitudes toward aging and retirement and, through case studies such as those used by Rosen and Jerdee (1985c), look at how they would actually treat an older person in a given situation. If time allows, a multicultural perspective on what aging means in several societies would help objectify the issue.

2. *Myths and Stereotypes of Growing Old.* Cognitive and experiential methodologies can be used here. Managers can identify common myths and stereotypes they have heard and seen at home, at work, and in the media since childhood about all minority groups, especially older persons. They need to look at what the potential effect of activating these false images is for the older person, for the company that employs him, and for the society at large. Accurate data — facts about older workers' learning abilities, productivity, and so on — should be provided to counteract the myths. A simulated sensory decline experience, for example, sitting for an hour with cotton in one's ears and trying to take notes on a lecture discussion, may help managers understand the physical, social, and emotional effects of having a sense deteriorate. Managers also need to develop action plans on how they can work to correct their own biases as well as those existing in their companies.

3. *Life Development and Changes.* It can be useful for managers to engage in a cursory study of developmental theories and their own life development over time. In this way, they can identify their own career and life phases, their developmental tasks, and their emotional and learning needs and compare them with those of a person over age fifty. Such reflection may help them identify value differences between them and older workers, especially the different meanings work may hold in one's life at a particular points in time. They may also come to appreciate how aspirations change with age and experience, how one accepts social role adjustments and other losses over time, and the growing significance of some kinds of rewards over others. As Davis and Taguri (1988, p. 129) remark in terms of life relationships, "harmony and conflict in a two-person relationship is a func-

tion of many factors, some influenced by the intersection of the two individuals' life stages."

4. *Dynamics of Workplace Interaction.* This aspect of the training should constitute the bulk of the time allotted for the program. Instructors need to use critical real-life incidents that occurred in the particular organization providing the learning. To make the sessions as practical as possible, they also need to use role-plays, minilectures, group discussions, videotaped cases, simulations, and skill practice opportunities. Older workers could be asked to describe problems they personally experienced and how these issues were dealt with by management. Among the subtopics (see Table 5) that may be addressed depending upon the unique requirements and needs of the particular company are:

A. *Communication skills* would include, for example, active listening, giving and receiving constructive feedback, facilitating team involvement of older adults, and mutual goal setting and problem solving by managers and workers of different generations.

B. *Motivational techniques* would include ideas about motivation mentioned earlier in this chapter.

C. *Stress and the older worker* would also address content previously discussed in this chapter.

D. *Age discrimination* would cover what it is, pertinent legal aspects, including information on the ADEA and its amendments, company policies, and how to make sure one is practic-

Table 5. Dynamics of Workplace Interaction: Subtopics.

A.	Communication skills
B.	Motivational techniques
C.	Stress and the older worker
D.	Age discrimination
E.	Learning and career development programs for older employees
F.	Conflict management
G.	Flexible leadership styles

ing age-neutral activities, especially in such areas as performance appraisal and promotions.

E. *Learning and career development programs for older employees* would incorporate suggestions from the literature and from corporate practice such as those described in earlier chapters of this book, especially ideas on learning programs for older workers and serial career planning.

F. *Conflict management* would direct managers to look closely at common sources of conflict that involve older workers, the effectiveness or ineffectiveness of conflict management techniques that have been used in the past, their own style of conflict management (avoidance, coercion, and so on), and its appropriateness for situations that involve individual older workers.

G. *Flexible leadership styles* would assess the manager's own leadership style and how it operates in certain situations through the use of instruments such as LEAD-Self and LEAD-Other (Hersey and Blanchard, 1988). Such tools enable managers to assess their own management style and compare their assessment with how others perceive it. It would focus on various theories of leadership such as the Tannenbaum and Schmidt Leadership Continuum, Path-Goal, Blake and Mouton's Managerial Grid, and various approaches to situational leadership to illustrate that there is no one right style for all situations at all times (Tannenbaum and Schmidt, 1958; House and Mitchell, 1974; Blake and Mouton, 1986; Hersey and Blanchard, 1988).

Participants in such a learning program would be exposed to the possibility of setting superordinate goals in intergenerational teams. Such an approach appeals to an older worker's organizational loyalty because it transcends petty differences and focuses on the good of the organization as a whole and how the team can work for its betterment. Such a module can also address the multicultural dimensions of a graying work force by presenting managers with a culture-based workplace problem and, in groups, evaluate how they handled it. For example, it might address the use of praise and recognition for someone whose sense of group is so strong it is a value not be set apart from it even in a "positive" way, as Americans would define it.

5. Action Planning. At the end of the learning series, managers may engage in a postlearning assessment of their attitudes toward aging, older adults, and so on, that had been pretested at the onset. They may wish also at this time to make an overall assessment of where their organization stands in policies, programs, and practices for mature employees. Then they can develop one or two action plans: the first for their own development in sensitivity to older worker issues, and the second for the corporation's growth in this arena.

Kaminski–da–Roza (1984) has described examples of action steps outlined in larger action plans that resulted from ten workshops conducted for 170 supervisors. Among the action steps identified by workshop participants were:

- Block out more frequent and regularly timed periods to sit down with an employee to listen and to give strokes and constructive feedback
- Work at goal setting and goal clarification with them, and in so doing make a concerted effort to find out what rewards are truly important to them
- Make better use of older workers' experience and expertise by involving them in special projects or using them as trainers or mentors
- Provide cross-training for older workers to keep them from getting burned out in repetitive, unstimulating jobs
- Secure their input into plans that affect them

Action planning relative to older workers will be discussed in more depth in Chapter Ten.

A significant segment of older workers is female. There are special and unique issues concerning them that need to be addressed. Chapter Nine looks at some of these learning issues and makes specific suggestions for programs for and about them.

Chapter 9

Older Women in the Work Force: Special Needs and Opportunities

Among the alterations we can anticipate in the work force of the year 2000 and beyond is its feminization. Women will be entering and remaining in the labor market in numbers that are expected to escalate at the same time that the percentage of white males in the labor force will be decreasing. HRD managers as well as heads of other organizational units will need to understand some of the issues germane to this growing and imposing presence of women, particularly women over age fifty, in corporate America. Between 1950 and 1987, midlife and older female workers doubled in number and are likely to reach, by the year 2000, 21 million—an increase of 7 million over 1987 ("Promoting Older Women's Employment Rights," 1988, p. 5). Herz (1988, p. 3) states that women aged fifty-five and older now constitute four out of ten older workers compared with two out of ten in 1950. This chapter treats matters of importance to managers who will supervise members of this group.

Women and Caregiving

As the demographics indicate, there is a steady increase in the "old-old" segment of the American population, that is, in the number of persons over age eighty-five. In the twenty-first century, the United States will rank behind only China and India in its percentage of older adults. The problems that corporations as a whole are experiencing in the 1990s with the need to care for the elderly population are indeed only the tip of the iceberg. More women are now working throughout their lifespan. Moreover, families for some time now have tended to have only one or two children. Clearly, there will have to be social agencies that provide support to midlife and older workers performing eldercare under a potentially great financial and emotional burden. The support might take such forms as *respite care,* that is, short-term relief, usually for a few hours, from complete responsibility for an aging adult. The Women's Bureau of the U.S. Department of Labor (1986b, p. 2) projects that, "because of longer life expectancies, rising median ages of the population and labor force, and delayed childbearing, an increasing proportion of women will be providing care to children under the age of eighteen as well as elderly relatives." A further complication is America's mobile life-style. Many of those persons involved in eldercare must bear the additional stress of orchestrating this care at a distance from their own geographic area.

Women, especially wives and daughters, have traditionally composed the vast majority of caregivers to older adults. Since the Women's Bureau, in the same publication, estimates that only about 10 percent of the 2.2 million persons who take care of a functionally impaired elderly person resign from their jobs, this tradition has great potential significance for companies in terms of productivity and job performance. There is no question but that responsibility for an elderly charge can impact work as much if not more than caring for a child; indeed, companies are only now beginning to look at its potential impact on organizational efficiency. Examples of the work-related effects include lost time due to phoning from work, absenteeism, and tardiness, as well as the necessity of rearranging schedules, reducing work hours, or taking time off without pay. *Working Age* ("Eldercare: The Emerging Employee Benefit," 1990) has discussed the findings of a one-year study conducted by *Fortune* magazine and John Hancock Financial Services of how corporate leaders and personnel are handling the eldercare matter. It showed that executives are becoming increasingly cognizant of how widespread problems of eldercare are among their employees, that such concerns and pressures affect productivity adversely, and that company policies are needed to help caregiving employees cope. The study also indicated that "female employees are more likely than male employees to have personal responsibility now or in the past two years for eldercare, and are more likely to anticipate quitting their jobs or taking time off for this purpose. . . . [They] are more likely to report stress and anxiety as side effects of elder caregiving" (p. 5).

Winfield (1987) has described how Elaine Cohen of Path-Finders, an eldercare organization that had developed workshops for Mobil Corporation and Consolidated Edison of New York, discovered that usually only a very sensitive and perceptive supervisor could detect that an employee had a problem with eldercare; companies in general finally became alerted to the problem when a longtime employee was placed in a crisis situation and might seek help through an employee relations or employee assistance program. Peterson and Rosenblatt (1986, p. 10) cite a poll by The Travelers Corporation of 739 employees revealing that "28 percent cared for an aged relative, spending an average of ten hours a week and doing so for an average of five years." Those surveyed described the effort as equivalent to assuming another full-time position.

Winfield (1987) mentions a study of three local firms by the University of Bridgeport's Aging Center showing that 25 percent of employees over age forty, primarily women, provided care for elderly persons; among the kinds of support given were housework, grocery shopping, meal preparation, giving medication, laundry, bathing, and dressing. Piktialis (1988) describes IBM's Elder Care consultation and referral service, developed after a survey of its employees revealed that 30 percent were responsible for some level of care for an elderly relative; through a network of 175 community organizations nationwide, the referral service acts as a clearinghouse of information about a wide variety of available eldercare services.

Organizations are increasingly recognizing the importance of eldercare in the lives of their employees and taking relevant actions. Among these firms is Champion International, a forest products and paper manaufacturing company in Stamford, Connecticut. Four types of assistance are made available to Champion's personnel:

1. Counseling for both employees and their aged dependents
2. *Caring for the Elderly,* an NCOA pamphlet that serves as a source of information and referral
3. A flexible benefits plan that provides for some eligible care of dependents to come out of pre-tax earnings
4. Unpaid leave for responsibilities related to eldercare up to a 180-day limit

The employee assistance program at Champion International provides information on the details of company policies ("Eldercare a Key Employee Benefit . . . ," 1987, p. 7).

Some other kinds of practices in which businesses and other agencies can engage to help their employees in caregiving are conducting lunchtime "brown bag" seminars on relevant topics; networking with community organizations to link them with employees; and setting up on-site day-care centers. Useful sources of information on existing programs and how to establish one in a company include AARP's Caregivers in the Workplace Program, which operates out of the association's Health Advocacy Services Division; for others, see the section on eldercare in Resources for Further Information, at the end of this book.

The effects of eldercare problems on working caregivers can be profound. Guilt, anger, frustration, and depression are among the emotional conditions this kind of stress can induce; moreover, they lead to outward manifestations such as chronic fatigue, migraine headaches, inability to sleep through the night, digestive disorders, and inattentive, distracted behavior. No wonder that, in a study of 510 caregivers who were responsible for older persons with memory problems, Duke University researchers found that "34 percent had resorted to tranquilizers and other mind-altering drugs to ease their emotional pain — more than four times the level of such drug use in the general population" (Peterson and Rosenblatt, 1986, p. 2).

Aging: A Women's Issue?

Is aging a "women's issue?" Those who maintain that it is point to the longevity of women, that is, approximately seventy-nine years of age, while at the same time they are much more likely than men to be growing old alone and poor. Women over fifty, especially, attribute their work force participation much more often to economic necessity than do men. The Older Women's League (1986, p. 1) has statistically demonstrated the growing disparity in the financial status of men and women over time: "In 1984 . . . among women aged forty-five to forty-nine, for example, median total income was $9,443 compared to $25,094 for men of the same age. Among women aged sixty-five or over, median total income fell to $6,020, compared to $10,450 for men." One needs also to take into consideration, when digesting these statistics, that earnings for black women are even less in later life. Interestingly, the Women's Bureau of the U.S. Department of Labor (1985, p. 2) has reported that even when factors such as education, experience, and continuity of work life are parallel between men and women the disturbing earnings discrepancy persists, that is, that even today a woman makes approximately sixty-nine cents for every dollar a man of similar background earns. And women are still unlikely to be found in the traditionally male occupations where, by law, they would earn the same salaries as their male peers. The conclusion the bureau reached is that "this variation is attributed to unmeasured factors such as discrimination, personal attitudes, and quality of education."

The female baby boomer at work in 2020 will be in a far better economic position than her counterpart of the 1990s. Current work-life patterns of women demonstrate that not only are their work-force participation rates higher but also that there is no longer a notable decline in those rates during childbearing years (Herz, 1988, p. 4; National Commission on Working Women, 1987). Yet, even here, one needs to consider the factor of divorce, after which a man may have more discretionary income than ever before, while a woman, who is more often left as the single parent, faces a diminishment of the financial resources she had been previously able to call upon (National Commission on Working Women, 1987). Such women, whose marriages ended in midlife, may experience a later life more similar to a woman of sixty in the 1990s than to her dual-income yuppie sisters. Closely related is the public issue, to which the Women's Bureau (1986a, p. 1) has called attention, of the increasing poverty rate among families headed by women: "Families maintained by women have a poverty rate which is three times that of all families and five times the rate for married couple families." This is a particularly serious issue for minority female heads of households.

Several factors account for today's older woman's less than desirable economic position. Women have tended as a group to cluster in low-paying, low-skill, low-status jobs with no career ladder, primarily in sales, plant, factory, and clerical areas. Accordingly, their Social Security income, which is based on past salary contributions, tends to be low — an especially crucial factor for those women for whom such payments are their only source of support. Lack of economic resources, a traditionally defined, familial "woman's place," and societal pressures against educating women to pursue leadership and nontraditional work roles have all contributed to keeping today's cohort of older women underrepresented in executive, managerial, and higher-paying professional positions. Moreover, their work experience tends to count for less than a man's because it has been gained in jobs that society undervalues. In its *Report on the Status of Midlife and Older Women in America,* the Older Women's League (1986, p. 4) describes the economic responsibilities of women over forty-five, that is, that they head 14 million households, one-third of which contain children under eighteen and about two-fifths someone over sixty-five. Corporations are increasingly recognizing the toll caregiving for an elderly relative can take on a worker, a situation discussed earlier in this chapter, as about 75 percent of such caregivers are women. Because of periodically interrupted work careers often due to raising children, women have earned much less than men cumulatively over time and only about 20 percent of women over age sixty-five currently receive pension income. In counterpoint to explanations of job segregation and lower earnings for women due to intermittent work lives, Meier (1986) maintains that the same conditions are found to exist when studies are based on men and women who have worked for similar total durations of time and had their work lives interrupted the same number of times. Glasse (1988, p. 2) believes that the seeds of economic hardship in later life have been planted for women much earlier, for "by the time a woman reaches forty-five, many of the distinguishing characteristics of this downwardly mobile syndrome are already evident in her life: from the pattern of low wages to the exclusion from pension plans."

Women suffer from the negative stereotyping of older workers by employers, as do men. Women must also deal, however, with valuation based on attractiveness, which for many Americans is inversely related to their age. Glasse (1988, p. 6) goes so far as to assert, "Age discrimination in employment is well in place by age thirty for women in many occupations." Thus ageism is, for women, compounded by subscription to the stereotype that men grow old gracefully but women age.

Many women may be returning to the work force after several years; therefore, their skills are likely to be rusty or outdated or they may be deficient in knowledge of and practice with new technology. For all these reasons, it may be hard for them to secure gainful employment. Overall, too, women have tended to be less educated than men. Yet, even when one considers the professional roles women have assumed, it is clear that they tend to be concentrated in the lower-paying types, that is, nursing, teaching, and librarianship. It needs to be noted further that even among educated women, inequities appear when their careers are compared to those of men of similar status — for example, only 10 percent of college and university full professors are women (Meier, 1986). Finally, because of their erratic and traditionally low-paying work histories, often in part-time or temporary work, their benefits, especially health coverage, are inadequate; *Working Age* ("Women in the Workplace," 1988, p. 4) reports that "about five million women between forty and sixty-five years old have no health insurance." These issues will also be those of many future older women; according to Glasse

(1988, p. 5), "most new employment opportunities do not provide pension and health care benefits."

Human Resource Development
and Older Women Workers

Women in general face blocks to opportunity at specific points that mark an employee's progress within an organization. These points occur at hiring or entry level, due to lack of education and job access; when a chance for promotion comes up; and when a choice needs to be made about retention or displacement ("Women in the Workplace," 1988, p. 6). Such obstacles are compounded for older women who may have never been in the work force or who have limited or outdated skills because of discontinuity in their work life. Since they join or rejoin the work force later in life, they have fewer long-term work contacts or mentors who can initiate them into the rules of corporate politics; therefore, their chances for career advancement are likely to be slimmer than those of men and younger women. They are also less likely to get the kinds of visible and significant work assignments that can highlight skill, accomplishment, and contribution to the company. At times of layoffs, mergers, and acquisitions, older female workers may be seen as not worth further investment in training, education, and development and thus as likely candidates for termination.

Nor can older women necessarily feel comfortable and more likely to be appreciated by a younger female boss. An older woman stuck in what she perceives to be a dead-end, unfulfilling job may resent a recent MBA whom she views as having received unearned opportunities in a historical time period more hospitable to women's career growth. She may think to herself or out loud to peers, What can this kid know? or, She hasn't paid her dues. If she has worked there some time, she may feel she knows how best matters should be handled for the sake of the company. The young female manager often has her own psychological issues to deal with in such an arrangement; she may feel that performance review with an older female subordinate is like criticizing her mother; moreover, she has few or no female role models with whom she can discuss her role conflict. Such a manager may also be annoyed because she believes the employee expects special treatment from her because she is another woman.

HRD managers, especially, can address the issues discussed in this chapter and thereby make a contribution both to their companies and to individual older female employees. Corporate learning programs can empower such women by providing content and process that confront the existence of ageist stereotypical mind-sets, updating skills to protect them against obsolescence and educating them to prepare them for job advancement. Some possible programs are outlined in Table 6; these variations on management training ideas described in the previous chapter can be adapted for both employees and managers, but the focus is on the older female worker.

1. Attitudinal Analysis. It is important here for both employee and manager to assess their own attitudes and feelings about growing older, especially what it means for a female; it would be especially useful for managers and employees to first meet separately and then share their perspectives. Participants would reflect on where they would place themselves in both the career and the life cycle. A particularly useful approach is to consider female images in movies, TV, and popular magazines, and how these may be transplanted to the workplace. Seltzer (1984, p. 31) has commented on the destructive and myth-making images of older women, from "little old ladies of considerable assertiveness asking 'Where's the beef?'" to Oil of Olay filling stations;

**Table 6. Older Female Worker:
Sample Corporate Learning Programs.**

1.	Attitudinal analysis
2.	Orientation and initial job training
3.	Career ladder education programming
4.	Communication issues in the workplace
5.	Education in new technology
6.	Retirement education

[from] stooped over old women suffering from arthritis, or osteo-porosis, to sexless, unattractive old women taking pain killers." Discussion of assessment results would center around not only male-female issues, but also the manager-subordinate dynamic.

2. Orientation and Initial Job Training. Such first learning ses-sions for the new worker need to spell out as clearly as possible the formal organization so that workers have some sense of where they fit in the overall structure and mission; women who have been out of the work force for a long time may be paired with a "buddy," a female worker who has been with the company a while, to show her the ropes. Part of the job preparation of these women might include assisting them in translating their prior life learning in paid, volunteer, or other nonpaid work into viable skills for their current positions. It might also in-clude some learning in terms of essential reading and writing. On-the-job training for their current work might aim at con-fidence building through the coach-instructor's calling attention to a specific type of knowledge they already possess, for exam-ple, familiarity with various types of audiovisual equipment and, wherever possible, calling upon it and building on it.

3. Career Ladder Education Programming. This would need to be customized to the needs of women returning to the labor force or entering it for the first time. For older women who have a longer work history at that company or at others, there would be a somewhat different emphasis. Both categories of women, however, are likely to need career counseling that involves a close look at their interests and skills with a view to matching them with current and anticipated positions in the organization. Such ongoing programming that addresses the needs of older women over time within the organization can ensure that they have a true career ladder with many rungs and do not wind up in low-paying, terminal jobs. The Roundtable on Older Women in the Workforce (1988) points out that level of educa-tion in technological skills, in particular, is clearly linked to their internal and external marketability.

4. Communication Issues in the Workplace. This type of learning program would be especially valuable for managers, but it
could be broadened to other employee groups, especially for
departments where communication is known to be a problem.
Topics might include sex-role socialization for both genders;
generational values of different age cohorts, including consideration of both male-female and female-female differences; and
similarities and differences between men's and women's concerns
as they age. With regard to the last topic, Kahne (1985, p. 11)
maintains that "women's lifetime rhythms, their work experience, and their economic status do have some unique qualities
that relate both to the multiple roles they perform and to in-
stitutional and labor market responses to them." Among these
"unique qualities" one could name such work-related issues as
the stresses of eldercare and what if any role the company should
play in such a matter; lack of mentors and role models, especially for older female workers; how best to channel the alleged
increasing assertiveness of older women into decision-making
and problem-solving activities at all levels; and the need for flexible work alternatives for mature workers in general, but particularly for older women as an income supplement.

The Roundtable on Older Women in the Workforce
(1988, p. 16) offered recommendations from six focus groups
of women over age fifty from both the public and private sectors; the groups emphasized the importance of education and
training for older women themselves and employers. They went
on to observe how important it was for companies to understand the psychological factors involved in older women working, which include "a desire for challenging work, a sense of
fulfillment, and the opportunity to meet people." All of these
factors need to be repesented in the light of their impact on the
nature and quality of organizational communication.

5. Education in New Technology. As mentioned above in item
3, older women feel this kind of education is essential for advancement of any kind. The Roundtable on Older Women in
the Workforce (1988, p. 17) specifically mentioned the importance of the context of learning to older women, especially the

chance to learn through doing and in an environment where participants were of all ages. The focus groups whose discussions formed the basis for this report suggested (p. 24) that older women should be used as peer instructors to reduce anxiety and to act as role models.

6. Retirement Education. This is especially significant given the description earlier in this chapter of the unfortunate financial plight of too many elderly women. Financial planning should constitute the core of these sessions; it should include clear exposition of the company's policies and benefits as well as of other opportunities for economic improvement, such as entrepreneurial endeavors. As Seltzer (1984, p. 34) aptly puts it, "Most old women don't expect rose gardens in old age, but they shouldn't have to accept the fertilizer either."

Chapter Ten makes suggestions for developing action plans within organizations to empower older female and male workers. It considers how to accomplish such planning at three levels: systemwide, departmental, and employee-centered.

Chapter 10

Human Resource
Action Planning for
Older Worker Issues

As the composition of the nation's work force changes, corporations will need to adapt their HRD programming accordingly.
Increasing percentages of females, blacks, and diverse ethnic
groups, together with a decrease in youth available for entry-
level jobs, will occur during an epoch when workers' skills will
obsolesce quickly due to the rapid pace of technological advance.
The situation is one that poses an opportunity for innovative
and creative program design. Training, education, and development of older workers is likely to become a high priority for
organizations as they meet the challenges of the new work force.
This chapter will consider basic steps in action planning as well
as some ways in which ideas for such planning may be supplied
by the organization, the manager, and the employee so as to
most effectively utilize older human resources.

Action planning is often used to facilitate the accomplishment of daily tasks. However, the approach to action planning
taken in this book (see Table 7) is that of mapping a route for
the accomplishment of longer-term, or one-year, goals. The
process includes the following steps:

1. Make a self-assessment in terms of attitudes, programs, poli-
    cies, and practices to identify gaps.
2. Estimate what you want your program, policies, and prac-
    tices to look like one year from now.

Table 7. Steps in Action Planning.

---

1. Take inventory/identify gaps
2. Project desired state of affairs
3. Set goal(s)
4. Set attainable, measurable objectives
5. Determine process to reach objectives, goal(s)
6. Conduct force field analysis of problems and resources
7. Identify appropriate evaluation techniques

---

3. Set a goal that is likely to be attainable one year from now, such as integrating content on managing older workers into all management programming.

4. Set defined and measurable short-term objectives, combining them with related activities that have specific deadlines leading to the accomplishment of both the objective and the overall goal. For instance, one might plan by two months from today to design the first of three training modules concerning mature employees.

5. Depending on the complexity of the goal, action planners may need to set up a chronological sequence, always relating back to the overall goal. For example, the sequence might begin: "In order to attain my program goal, the objectives I must accomplish in the following *week* are . . . " This might be followed by "In order to attain my program goal, the objectives I must accomplish in the following *month* are . . . ," and then by "In order to accomplish my program goal, the objectives I must accomplish in the following *six months* are . . . ," and so on.

6. For each of the program objectives, planners need to conduct a mini force field analysis, looking at the forces operating to both foster and thwart successful outcomes.

7. Additionally, for each objective, it is helpful to assess, besides anticipated *problems* (such as cost and staff time) and available *resources* (such as an HRD program specialist with a certificate in gerontology): (1) what additional *support* might be available — for example, through grant funding — and (2) what *techniques* will be used to *measure* progress on an ongoing basis.

Action Planning by and for the Organization

Like managers and employees, the organization as a whole needs to begin the process of action planning with a self-inventory. At the organizational level, appropriate goal setting must start with taking stock of where the company is now with regard to its attitudes, policies, and practices concerning older workers. Moreover, the more top management and the norms of the current corporate culture are supportive of older workers, the greater is the likelihood that effective action plans will ensue and be implemented.

A great many areas are ripe for review and subsequent action planning at the corporate level. Among them are "age-neutral" recruiting, retention, and promotion activities, especially performance appraisals, and termination practices. There needs to be an awareness at all levels of what constitutes age discrimination. At the same time, information about what constitutes nonexclusive behavior should be readily available. Management should examine current benefit packages to make sure they are equitable. In particular, it will have to explore the tradeoffs between such variables as the expense of health benefits for part-time workers and the real but intangible returns, such as enhanced companywide morale and the quality service often associated with loyal "seasoned" staff.

In order to set up the kinds of programs we reviewed in Chapters Four and Five, the indispensable first step is to audit what alternatives could be expanded and adapted to fit the needs of other workers, especially younger women with families who wish to stay in the work force. This audit will not be meaningful without a parallel one of what services or referrals the company provides for workers with regard to day care for younger persons and eldercare for children of aging parents.

Having identified the work options and the related needs for training, the company should review the content and process of all learning programs to make sure that they are elder-friendly and that a philosophy of investment in the older employee is in effect. Career programming based on actual career ladders with rungs for older adults should be instituted (see Chapter Seven).

Programs for older workers will not succeed if ageist attitudes are allowed to persist. It is therefore essential to assess management attitudes toward older workers and to debunk ageist myths and stereotypes. Surveys designed for this purpose have been sponsored by the AARP; information about them can be obtained from its Worker Equity Department.

On the financial side, it will pay to examine the current corporate attitude toward early retirement in order to gauge its long-term costs to the company and to compare those against the benefits of rehiring employees or extending their work lives. The company should also consider its pension plans to see if modifications are needed to allow retirees to work for the company without losing pension benefits and also to make sure that there are not built-in biases against women, particularly older ones (see Chapter Nine).

Finally, as part of its long-term action plan, the company could audit the total number of its personnel age forty and over, as well as the kinds and levels of positions they occupy. In this way it would obtain an accurate *age profile* of the company for decision-making purposes. One might then use this information to see not only how many older workers there are overall and what departments and positions they occupy but also how much influence they exert in the system — a *power profile,* in short. Having done so, it would be a logical next step to arrange opportunities for older workers to identify problems that currently exist in the company relative to them and to offer recommendations about new directions for older-worker programs, policies, and practices.

Action Planning by and for Managers

All managers need to assess their own attitudes toward and factual knowledge of the physiological and psychosocial dynamics of aging (see Chapter Three). If a supervisor truly believes that someone over age fifty is set in his ways and resistant to change, why should she place him on a task force on converting from manual to automated systems? Ageist beliefs are also likely to translate into behaviors such as restricting participation of older workers in new ventures engaged in by the corporation.

Part of this managerial self-examination, as we just saw, needs to include comparing one's own behaviors with those of the organization as a whole. For example, a manager could ask himself, "How are my actions contributing to an age-neutral climate with regard to programs, policies, and procedures in my department?"

Action planning by HRD managers for their older employees is a major avenue to addressing the organizational priority of training, educating, and developing older employees. Essentially, HRD managers will need to:

1. Take an inventory of what, in their existing learning programs, already speaks to older-worker issues
2. Identify what gaps occur in those learning programs and assess what content and process would be most appropriate to fill in those gaps
3. Consider not only what is needed but also how to accomplish it effectively and efficiently
4. Keep in mind that older-worker programming would involve learning efforts directed not only at older workers themselves but also at senior management, supervisors directly responsible for mature employees, and other company personnel, including HRD staff

Kaminski–da–Roza (1984) discusses an action planning program that had two goals: maximizing the contributions of mature employees and integrating them constructively into an organization. She points out that the line managers in a large R & D laboratory identified training as one area for taking long-term actions, which she defined (p. 52) as "those that require some preparation to begin and that will take longer than a year." Among the intended means of achieving one or both of the two aforementioned goals were helping older workers specify their career objectives and provide themselves with relevant education—for example, in technology; making use of older adults as trainers in a mentoring or master-apprentice relationship; reviewing off-site education with an eye toward making sure older workers were receiving their fair share; implementing cross-training for older personnel; and sorting out the myths from the realities of aging.

HRD departments can contribute to the cultivation of an effective multigenerational work force through relevant adult learning programs set in the context of action plans as already described in this section. There are at least five types of programs to be considered:

1. Programs for the older worker
2. Programs for managers on older-worker issues
3. Programs for senior management on older-worker issues
4. Programs for HRD staff
5. Programs for employees in general

Programs for the Older Worker. Obviously, there is a need for programs relating directly to older workers' job skills. Such programs should include:

- Periodic skills updating to prevent obsolescence and make opportunities for promotion more likely
- Education for prospective new jobs within the company
- Education in new technology and processes
- Preretirement education, including preparation for second careers
- Occupational education for older persons likely to be replaced by automation

To stop there, however, would be to seriously undervalue older workers as a resource. They also merit career ladder presentations that elucidate optional routes for upward mobility within the organization. A key component here is *presupervisory learning* aimed at older workers who in later life may wish to explore opportunities in supervision but who first need to have a better idea of what such commitment involves. Also beneficial is training in memory enhancement strategies, which can be incorporated in the learning designs of other programs or established as a program in its own right.

An entire constellation of learning programs centered on the attributes of the new worker can make it more likely that older persons will secure meaningful and responsible roles in the evolving work force. These include programs in customer relations, problem solving, stress management, and mutual goal setting. In addition, development programs can help clarify basic values, such as what place and meaning work holds in the older employee's life at this point, and thus improve motivation by establishing what rewards are currently most appropriate.

Programs for Managers on Older-Worker Issues. All managers should become familiar with the demographic changes in the country and in the company and with the composition of the organization's personnel that is likely to result from current trends. Management education, as outlined in Chapter Eight, should include understanding the legal climate of age discrimination and the changes in values, developmental tasks, and physique older workers are experiencing due to their particular stage in the life cycle. They should be thoroughly familiar with the pros and cons of various alternative job options and how they could benefit not only older workers but also other segments of the company's work force. Younger managers, especially, should study communication styles and strategies that will create a positive motivational climate for older workers. Managerial self-assessment, above all for receptivity to a participative style, stereotypes, and openness to change and group diversity, is a valuable starting point for these exercises.

With this background, managers could proceed to study the characteristics of current older workers and how to constructively make use of such qualities of theirs as familiarity with the company and its personnel, rules, and so on; their loyalty to it; and their strong work ethic. Such programming should also indicate the shifts that are likely to occur when the baby boomers come of age and form a large group of older persons who are more assertive and better educated. Study at this level should include such vital but easily neglected details as the adaptations in the work environment that may become necessary as the company's work force ages. For example, care should be taken that temperature is modulated; that there is full-spectrum lighting (or at least sufficient lighting with reduced glare); that there is not overwhelming sensory overload; and that employees need not bend, stoop, or engage in prolonged heavy work.

Given the magnitude of the issues, it is important that managers' perspective on them should not be confined to the companies in which they work. Knowledge of what age-neutral or older-worker policies and practices other companies have adopted—for example, with regard to recruitment, hiring, placement, promotion, and retirement and pensions—will help them generate ideas of their own. Naturally, they should also review company policies with a view to altering them if they are found to be prejudicial. Of particular relevance here are issues specifically related to older female workers, including such issues as pay inequity and the burden of caregiving.

Programs for Senior Management on Older-Worker Issues. As the strong commitment of top managers is crucial, though not essential, for the initiation and implementation of older-worker programming, selected learning sessions should be made available to them. Among the aforementioned programs for managers that could be helpful are those dealing with current demographic trends in nation and company, the contributions older workers can bring to an organization, and review of the company's older-worker policies and practices in light of what other companies are doing. It would be instructive to add a brainstorming component allowing for the generation of suggestions on older-worker needs.

Programs for HRD Staff. HRD personnel should become conversant with all of the above topic areas and then specialize in a few. As educators and trainers, they need to be aware of the learning characteristics of adult learners, and of older workers in particular. Among these characteristics are more of an orientation to self-paced than to strictly timed instruction, more frequent breaks, and a decline in sensory and other physiological functioning that should be compensated for by adjustments in the work environment and by special instructional materials. Older adults need a supportive climate for learning — for example, the encouragement and reinforcement provided by the job coach in McDonald's educational programming — to ameliorate likely feelings of inadequacy because of rusty skills or fear of competition with younger workers. They do better in sequenced learning sessions built on what is already known or experienced and in hands-on or simulated learning that gives them a chance to practice and master the tasks before being called on in the work situation.

As in all learning, two-way communication counts for much. Older workers need an opportunity for input into the design of learning programs. They also need to be taught in small groups, to reduce the anxiety of being called on for the "right" answer, and to be provided with ongoing communication, particularly feedback on performance and recognition for achievement by supervisor or coach. The learning sessions themselves should incorporate memory enhancement activities, new knowledge and skills directly applicable to the work situation, and opportunities for mutual goal setting and reward definition in which the purposes and goals of education are clearly delineated. The sessions should not be segregated by age, or at the least they should be combined with programs in which older workers learn with other employee groups. Older workers should be used as trainers in such sessions as well as in mentor roles (see Chapter Six).

Programs for Employees in General. Selected programming for personnel could contribute to a work environment in which older workers are seen as a positive and viable force — a more enriching environment in general. Among the types of programs that could be used here are programs on:

- Self-assessment in attitudes toward aging
- Awareness of myths and realities of the aging process
- External and internal demographic changes

- Characteristics of older learners, especially related to learning capabilities
- Appropriate communication processes and skills

Action Planning by and for the Employee

According to estimates by work-force analysts, between 75 percent and 90 percent of those who will be workers in the year 2000 are already in the work force today. What characteristics and qualities will these "new" workers need — and how can HRD ensure mature employees will fit the bill? This section will explore both questions.

Attributes of the New Worker. Given the combination of high technology and high commercial competition, it seems likely that the new worker will need a concern for quality and for satisfying the customer, with the motivation and ability to continuously retool job-related skills. The definition of what is a job-related skill will be expanded. This worker will be capable of working somewhat autonomously without close supervision in various locations. She or he will know and practice cooperative group skills as member, facilitator, and leader and will have a sense of responsibility great enough to carry out tasks under a supervisor who is more of a coach than a controller.

Workers will also tend to be better educated. They will need a solid grounding in the fundamentals of reading, writing, computation, logical thinking for analysis and problem solving, and computer literacy. More valuable even than all these will be the ability to engage in self-directed learning, especially that involving instructional technology and knowing what information one needs to have and how to get it. These workers, far from resisting change, will accept that it is normal and will welcome unique situations with no precedents or past frames of reference to guide them. Since they will be capable of learning sophisticated concepts and high-level skills, they will also be capable of planning, of setting goals for themselves and for the project team in cooperation with others. In general, they will be attuned to originality, synthesis of others' ideas, and piggybacking on the contributions of other members of the group.

In conclusion, virtually all workers in the year 2000 will need to cultivate a range of qualities previously required of only a few. Among them will be (1) sensitivity toward and appreciation of cultural, gender, racial, and age differences and (2) demonstration of these qualities in interpersonal communication on the job. A capacity for high productivity, too, will be indispensable, especially in the service sector, where this trait will be of growing significance. The most effective workers will be the ones who care about and show concern for the other people in the organization, from those in units at their own level to the CEO and the board of directors, as part of one holistic organizational team.

Tapping the Potential of Older Workers. Can an older worker match these characteristics of an effective work force of the twenty-first century? Clearly the potential is there. Whether it is actualized depends in rather large measure on what Nadler (1984, sec. 1.144) deem the "unique contribution of HRD"— that is, learning. According to the results of a 1982 Harris survey conducted for the NCOA, as cited by the National Commission for Employment Policy (1985, p. 23), the interest exists among older workers: "Fifty-six percent of respondents aged fifty-five to sixty-four were taking or had recently completed educational courses to acquire marketable job skills."

Older workers often underestimate their influence on the corporation for positive change. Some managers believe that these employees are reluctant to engage in training programs and that they experience resistance to or, at the very least, anxiety about the use of new technology. Mature workers can alter these beliefs by taking constructive action. They can begin by assessing their own attitudes and behaviors about growing older to determine if, in fact, they themselves buy into or reinforce the myths and stereotypes about aging (see Chapter One). They can also cooperate in reviewing HRD programming to make sure that it provides accurate content about older workers and that, when directed at them, it uses the basic principles of educating them that we reviewed in Chapter Six.

Older workers should also consider becoming involved, where the corporate environment is hospitable to it, in task forces that engage in organizational diagnosis and action planning at the system-wide level. This is just one of the ways in which they can make clear to management that some older workers *want* to be "invested in" with regard to retooling of skills, promotional opportunities, and so on. However, it is not enough to raise the consciousness of management that aging adults are or can be motivated. Management has to be told that, if older workers are to be motivated, their rewards should match their career and life stage. This is only one respect in which managers need to be trained in responding to older human resources as persons continually maturing, changing, and growing (see Chapter Three).

There are in fact many ways in which older workers can foster an awareness within a company of the particular advantages to it (for example, lower turnover) of maintaining and reemploying older workers. Not least among these benefits, given the anticipated problems with the lack of basic skills among younger workers in the year 2000, is a solid grounding in literacy. But the most persuasive argument of all is personal example. By participating in training, education, and development activities, they can become living proof that older adults can indeed learn — and learn well.

Finally, older workers should not hesitate to become members of older-adult advocacy, information and referral, and service organizations, such as the National Council on the Aging and the American Association of Retired Persons, and become conversant with older-worker issues. A descriptive list of such organizations and the resources they offer will be found at the end of this book in the section headed Resources for Further Information.

The Older Worker: Employee of the Future

Would there be sufficient return on investment for companies offering learning to older workers and about older-worker issues? Clearly the answer is yes. As we saw earlier, a newly hired fifty-year-old worker is likely to remain with the company approximately fifteen years, while someone between twenty and thirty may stay with that company three to five years. Moreover, given the rapidity of technological change, a fifty-year-old employee's remaining years with the organization will outlast any new technology in which the employee would undergo education.

As this book has pointed out repeatedly, current research studies document a case for older-worker employment. So does the actual experience of companies in the vanguard of adapting to changing demographics. Long-range statistical projections point to the need for rethinking the role of aging employees and reevaluating the impact of retirement on the individual, the company, and society. The data are there. The need is there. The challenge is there.

In my opinion, what must occur is a shift in mind-set from still prevalent ageist beliefs to a more realistic assessment of what older employees can contribute to organizations as they enter the twenty-first century. As a group, older workers are valuable and viable human resources. With changing demographics, they are likely to become needed resources as well. They bring to a job and to an organization vast reservoirs of life experiences for use in judgment calls, problem solving, and conflict resolution. They bring loyalty, commitment, coping skills, responsibility, capacity to learn, and interest in working and in offering a fair day's work for a fair day's pay.

As an "age wave" (Dychtwald, 1989) moves across America, employers who have not felt the need to be informed, imaginative and open with regard to older workers may need to consider extending the work lives of mature workers and rehiring retirees through varied alternative work options. As jobs become less physically demanding, physical deficits become less of a factor. The emphasis is then more on what skills and abilities workers retain than on what they may have lost. Investing in the older worker is an investment in the organization. Workers who are retooled with new skills remain with the company that trained them. Moreover, the interaction between younger and older workers can be a symbiotic one. As companies like Control Data have found, older workers can serve as role models and mentors, showing the ropes to novices in the corporate culture. Conversely, someone new to the organization can bring fresh ideas from the outside that trigger creative adaptations in the minds of veteran employees. Too often, plateaued careers, job burnout, and skill obsolescence, which eventuate in talent drain and are costly to the company financially and in terms of morale, result from the firm not following enlightened, age-neutral policies.

As Dychtwald (1989, pp. 183–184) states: "Older workers don't want to punch the clock, would like a better blend of work and play, usually want to collaborate with intergenerational teams, and want to be more appreciated for their unique skills and experience." In other words, they have *human* needs for freedom, dignity, variety, communication, respect, and recognition. They are us — just at a different point in time. And the new rules about older workers — and older managers — that we put in place today may be those that will determine the fate of our own work lives. As we ride the crest of the age wave, let us not forget that we are in this boat together.

Resources for
Further Information:
Organizations and
Publications

Organizations

The following lists of organizations and programs are not intended to be exhaustive, but they do include most of those doing significant work at the national level. I have tried to indicate which ones represent or offer information on older-worker as distinct from older-adult interests, but of course the line is frequently hard to draw. I have also included more detailed information about two outstanding national programs for older workers.

Selected Resource Organizations

Aging in America
1500 Pelham Parkway South
Bronx, N.Y. 10461

Provides programs and services to enhance the quality of life for older persons; these include the Projects with Industry program to facilitate the reentry of older persons into the work force.

American Association of Retired Persons
1909 K Street NW
Washington, D.C. 20049

Publishes *Modern Maturity* (free to members) and acts as a source of general information. Its Worker Equity Department, in the division of Business Partnerships, publishes the journal *Working Age* and operates the National Older Worker Information System (NOWIS), which updates information on companies using older workers in a variety of creative jobs. Other agencies of the AARP that could provide useful information for HRD sessions include The Women's Initiative and the Institute of Lifetime Learning. The National Gerontology Resource Center, which is the library of the association, offers very useful information to members and to legitimate researchers. The AARP also operates a data base called Ageline that provides information specifically on matters relating to older adults.

American Society on Aging
833 Market Street
San Francisco, Calif. 94103

Through its Training Center on Aging, the ASA also provides continuing education in relevant fields. Publishes *Generations* and operates ASA Answers, an information service.

Center for Social Gerontology
117 N. First Street
Ann Arbor, Mich. 48104

Produces films and other resources of an educational nature; the center also provides consultation services, produces research reports, and offers conferences.

Gerontological Society of America
1411 K Street NW
Washington, D.C. 20005

Publishes *The Gerontologist* and the *Journal of Gerontology.*

National Center and Caucus on the Black Aged, Inc.
1424 K Street NW
Washington, D.C. 20005

Seeks to enhance the status of all elderly Americans, especially blacks; runs an employment program that exists in eleven states.

National Council on the Aging
600 Maryland Avenue SW
Washington, D.C. 20004

Publishes *Perspective on Aging* and *Current Literature on Aging,* which
provide topical information to members. The council also sponsors the National Association of Older Worker Employment Services (NAOWES) and the Prime Time Productivity Program,
which work to promote the use of older workers. The Prime
Time Productivity Program publishes *The Aging Workforce,* a
review of trends in the hiring, retention, and training of both
middle-aged and older workers. The NCOA has developed training programs and materials for older adults reentering the work
force, as well as for agencies that wish to understand the myths
about and characteristics of aging. The National Center for
Health Promotion and Aging, a unit of the NCOA, provides
training and information on health promotion programs as well
as a library.

Office of Human Development Services
U.S. Department of Health and Human Services
200 Independence Avenue SW
Washington, D.C. 20201

Publishes *Aging,* a quarterly magazine.

Older Women's League
730 11th Street NW
Washington, D.C. 20001

Source of information and educational materials on matters of
concern to middle-aged and older women. Also provides a
speakers' bureau.

Research Centers and Sources of Research Studies

Employment and Retirement Division
Andrus Gerontology Center
University of Southern California
P.O. Box 77912
Los Angeles, Calif. 90007

Produces publications on employment issues related to older adults.

Institute of Gerontology
University of Michigan
300 North Ingalls Street
Ann Arbor, Mich. 48109

Conducts research on topics of importance to older adults.

Programs of Note

Prime Time Productivity
National Council on the Aging

According to my interview in July 1988 with Dean Hewitt, program director, this is an important program resource for companies. It publishes a bimonthly bulletin, *Corporate Newsline,* that offers practical hints to enhance programs for older workers, and *Aging Workforce,* a quarterly. It also hosts conferences and offers consulting, program development, and training services that are individually tailored to a business's needs. Examples of such activities, all intended to make the most efficient use of the skills and talents of middle-aged and older workers, are:

- Taking preventive measures with regard to age discrimination lawsuits
- Training managers to adopt age-neutral practices
- Creating job-sharing opportunities
- Establishing linkages with local, state, and national programs that recruit and train middle-aged and older workers

Funded by the U.S. Department of Labor with support from Exxon, Chevron, and AT&T, Prime Time Productivity offers training and consultation that has long-term human service implications.

Worker Equity Initiative
American Association of Retired Persons

According to my interview in July 1988 with Bernard Nash, director of the AARP's Division of Business Partnerships, the Worker Equity Initiative aims to work with and educate businesses so that they will hire, retain, and make constructive use of older employees; to adopt and implement age-neutral policies and practices; and to heighten public awareness of older workers' actual, not stereotypical, capabilities and also of their needs and rights. In addition to surveys and research studies on older workers, the program publishes *Working Age,* a bimonthly newsletter offering up-to-date information on older-employee matters; manages the NOWIS data base on specific programs, such as types of alternative work options, currently in use by organizations; and provides speakers and exhibits for conferences and so forth.

Publications

The following is a topical list of references on subjects of interest to managers and HRD professionals concerned about older-worker issues. These topics are either not treated in depth in this book or call attention to additional sources not directly referred to in the narrative. The works listed have been selected for a combination of two or more of these factors: readability, practical bent, relevance, authoritativeness, and comparative recency of publication. When items are included that were published several years ago, it is because they have an enduring usefulness for today's manager.

I recommend that all supervisors of older workers first become familiar with the resources available through organizations such as those described early in this resource. After achieving a general knowledge of what is available, they can move on to the specialized topics below.

Aging and Human Development

Aiken, L. R. *Later Life.* (3rd ed.) Hillsdale, N.J.: Erlbaum, 1989.
Atchley, R. *Social Forces and Aging.* (5th ed.) Belmont, Calif.: Wadsworth, 1989.

Belenky, M. F., Clinchy, B. M., Goldberger, N. R., and Tur-
ule, J. M. *Women's Ways of Knowing.* New York: Basic Books,
1986.
Cox, H. *Later Life.* Englewood Cliffs, N.J.: Prentice-Hall, 1984.
Gould, R. *Transformations: Growth and Change in Adult Life.* New
York: Simon & Schuster, 1978.
Havighurst, R. J. *Developmental Tasks and Education.* New York:
McKay, 1973.
Hooyman, N. R., and Kiyak, H. A. *Social Gerontology: A Multi-
disciplinary Perspective.* Newton, Mass.: Allyn & Bacon, 1988.
Levinson, D. J. *The Seasons of a Man's Life.* New York: Knopf,
1978.
Neugarten, B. L. "Adaptation and the Life Cycle." *Counseling
Psychologist,* 1976, *6,* 16–20.
Neugarten, B. L. "Time, Age and the Life Cycle." *American Jour-
nal of Psychology,* 1979, *136,* 887–894.
Santrock, J. W. *Adult Development and Aging.* Dubuque, Iowa:
Brown, 1985.
Vaillant, G. E. *Adaptation to Life.* Boston: Little, Brown, 1977.
Viorst, J. *Necessary Losses.* New York: Ballantine Books, 1987.

Age Discrimination in Employment

Album, M. J. "Controversy over Waivers Under the Age Discrimination in Employment Act Continues." *Employment Relations Today,* Winter 1988–89, *15,* 347–350.
American Association of Retired Persons, *The Legal ABC's of Hir-
ing Older Workers.* Washington, D.C.: American Association
of Retired Persons, 1989.
"Employer Liable Under ADEA If Age Is a Factor." *Employee
Benefit Plan Review,* 1988, *42* (Feb.), 43–44.
Levine, M. L. *Age Discrimination and the Mandatory Retirement Controversy.* Baltimore, Md.: Johns Hopkins University Press,
1988.
Singer, M. S., and Sewell, C. "Applicant Age and Selection
Interview Decisions: Effect of Information on Exposure on
Age Discrmination in Personnel Selection." *Personnel Psychol-
ogy,* 1989, *42,* 135–154.

U.S. Congress. Senate. Special Committee on Aging. *Twenty Years of the Age Discrimination in Employment Act: Success or Failure?* 100th Cong., 1st sess., Sept. 10, 1987.

Alternative Work Options

American Association of Retired Persons. *Using the Experience of a Lifetime.* Washington, D.C.: American Association of Retired Persons, 1988.

Axel, H. *Job Banks for Retirees.* New York: The Conference Board, 1989.

Fyock, C. D. *Making the Older Worker Connection: Your Complete Guide to Facts, Figures, Names, Addresses, and Phone Numbers to Make Your Company's Older Worker Program a Success.* Louisville, Ky.: Innovative Management Concepts, 1988.

Humple, C. S., and Lyons, M. *Management and the Older Workforce: Policies and Programs.* New York: American Management Association, 1983.

Lee, P. *The Complete Guide to Job Sharing.* New York: Walker, 1983.

McConnell, S. R. "Alternative Work Patterns for an Aging Work Force." In P. Ragan (ed.), *Work and Retirement: Policy Issues.* Los Angeles: University of Southern California Press, 1980.

National Alliance of Business. *Invest in Experience: New Directions for an Aging Workforce.* Washington, D.C.: National Alliance of Business, 1985.

Olmsted, B. *Creating a Flexible Workplace: How to Select and Manage Alternative Work Options.* New York: American Management Association, 1989.

Public/Private Partnerships in Aging: A Compendium. Washington, D.C.: National Association of State Units on Aging / Washington Business Group on Health, 1987.

Rhine, S. H. *Managing Older Workers: Company Policies and Attitudes.* New York: The Conference Board, 1984.

Robinson, P. K. *Organizational Strategies for Older Workers.* Elmsford, N.Y.: Pergamon Press, 1983.

Root, L. S. "Corporate Programs for Older Workers." *Aging,* 1985, *351,* 12–16.

Stackel, L. "More and More Companies Are Recruiting and Retraining Older, Retired Workers to Meet Their Employment Needs." *Employment Relations Today,* 1988, *15,* 72-77.

Career Development and Management

Bardwick, J. *The Plateauing Trap.* New York: AMACOM, 1986.
Brown, D., Brooks, L., and Associates. *Career Choice and Development: Applying Contemporary Theories to Practice.* San Francisco: Jossey-Bass, 1984.
Gutteridge, T. G., and Hutcheson, P. G. "Career Development." In L. Nadler (ed.), *The Handbook of Human Resource Development.* New York: Wiley, 1984.
Kauffman, N. "Motivating the Older Worker." *Advanced Management Journal,* 1987, *52,* 43-48.
London, M., and Mone, E. M. *Career Growth and Human Resource Strategies.* Westport, Conn.: Quorum, 1988.
Mattone, J. *Positive Performance Management: A Guide to "Win-Win" Reviews.* Shawnee Mission, Kans.: National Press Publications, 1988.
Olson, S. K. (ed.). "Career Counseling of Older Adults: Special Issue." *Journal of Career Development,* 1986, *13*(2) entire issue.
Sonnenfeld, J. *The Hero's Farewell: What Happens When CEOs Retire.* New York: Oxford University Press, 1988.
Sonnenfeld, J., and Kotter, J. P. "The Maturation of Career Theory." *Human Relations Journal,* 1982, *35,* 19-46.

Characteristics of Older Workers

American Association of Retired Persons. *Workers Over 50: Old Myths, New Realities.* Washington, D.C.: American Association of Retired Persons, 1986.
Doering, M., Rhodes, S., and Schuster, M. *The Aging Worker: Research and Recommendations.* Newbury Park, Calif.: Sage, 1983.
The Older Worker. Madison, Wis.: Industrial Relations Research Association, 1988.
Predictors of Success Among Older Workers in New Jobs. Gorham, Maine: University of Southern Maine, 1989.

Rupp, K., Bryant, E. C., Mantovani, R. E., and Rhoads, M. D. *Factors Affecting the Participation of Older Americans in Employment and Training Programs.* Washington, D.C.: National Commission for Employment Policy, n.d.

Compensation and Benefits

American Association of Retired Persons. *Today's Careers, Tomorrow's Pensions: A Pension Portability Analysis Executive Summary.* Washington, D.C.: American Association of Retired Persons Public Policy Institute, 1988.

Corporate Benefits Plans: International and Domestic Perspectives. Brookfield, Wis.: International Foundation of Employee Benefit Plans, 1988.

"The Impact of Recent ADEA Changes on Employee Benefit Plans." *Employment Relations Law Journal,* 1987, *13,* 154–163.

Paul, R. D. *The Sourcebook on Postretirement Health Care Benefits.* Greenvale, N.Y.: Panel, 1988.

Sahin, I. *Health Care Benefits for Retirees: A Framework for Measurement.* Brookfield, Wis.: International Foundation of Employee Benefit Plans, 1988.

Eldercare

Anastas, J. W. *Breadwinners and Caregivers: Interviews with Working Women.* Washington, D.C.: National Association of Area Agencies on Aging, 1987.

Creedon, M. *Eldercare: A Resource Guide.* Bridgeport, Conn.: Center for the Study of Aging, University of Bridgeport, for PepsiCo, 1986.

Creedon, M. *Issues for An Aging America: Employees and Eldercare.* Washington, D.C.: National Council for the Aging, 1987.

"Eldercare Is an Emerging Employee Benefit." *The Aging Workforce,* 1988, *2*(2), 3.

Employers and Eldercare: A New Benefit Coming of Age. Washington, D.C.: Bureau of National Affairs, 1988.

Gibeau, J. L. *Breadwinners and Caregivers: Supporting Workers Who Care for Elderly Family Members: Final Report, Executive Summary.*

Washington, D.C.: National Association of Area Agencies on Aging, 1987.

Kenny, J., and Spicer, S. *Eldercare: Coping with Later Life Stresses.* Buffalo, N.Y.: Prometheus Books, 1989.

Winfield, F. E. "Workplace Solutions for Women Under Eldercare Pressure." *Personnel Journal,* 1987, *64*(7), 31–39.

General Interest

Axel, H. (ed.). *Employing Older Americans: Opportunities and Constraints.* New York: The Conference Board, 1988.

Bluestone, I. (ed.). *The Aging of the American Work Force: Problems, Programs, Policies.* Detroit, Mich.: Wayne State University Press, 1989.

Butler, R. (ed.). *Productive Aging.* New York: Springer, 1985.

Dennis, H. (ed.) *Fourteen Steps in Managing an Aging Workforce.* Lexington, Mass.: Heath, 1988.

Dychtwald, K. *Age Wave: The Challenges and Opportunities of an Aging America.* Los Angeles: Tarcher, 1989.

Greller, M. K. *From Baby Boom to Baby Bust: How Business Can Meet the Demographic Challenge.* Reading, Mass.: Addison-Wesley, 1989.

Johnson, W. B., and Packer, A. H. *Workforce 2000: Work and Workers for the Twenty-First Century.* Indianapolis, Ind.: Hudson Institute, 1987.

Rosen, B., and Jerdee, T. H. *Older Employees: New Roles for Valued Resources.* Homewood, Ill.: Irwin, 1985.

Sandell, S. (ed.). *The Problem Isn't Age: Work and Older Americans.* New York: Praeger, 1987.

Worker Equity Department, American Association of Retired Persons. *How to Manage Older Workers.* Washington, D.C.: American Association of Retired Persons, 1988.

Human Resource Development

Barocas, V. S. *Employment and Training of the Mature Worker: A Training Design.* Washington, D.C.: National Council on the Aging, 1982.

Bove, R. "Retraining the Older Worker." *Training and Development Journal,* 1987, *41,* 76–78.

Casner-Lotto, J., and Associates. *Successful Training Strategies: Twenty-Six Innovative Corporate Models.* San Francisco: Jossey-Bass, 1988.

Lester, B. *A Practitioner's Guide for Training Older Workers.* Washington, D.C.: National Commission for Employment Policy, 1984.

Nadler, L., and Nadler, Z. *Developing Human Resources: Concepts and a Model.* (3rd ed.) San Francisco: Jossey-Bass, 1989.

Odiorne, G. "Managing GRAMPIES." *Training,* 1988, *25*(6), 37–39.

Peterson, D. A. *Facilitating Education for Older Learners.* San Francisco: Jossey-Bass, 1983.

Rosen, B., and Jerdee, T. H. "Investing in the Older Worker." *Personnel Administrator,* 1989, *34*(4), 70–72, 74.

Taylor, S. "The Aging of America." *Training and Development Journal,* 1989, *43*(10), 44–52.

Worker Equity Department, American Association of Retired Persons. *How to Train Older Workers.* Washington, D.C.: American Association of Retired Persons, 1988.

The Job Training Partnership Act (JTPA) and Programs

Alegria, F. L., and Lordeman, A. *Serving Older Individuals Under the Job Training Partnership Act: State Initiatives and Practices.* Washington, D.C.: National Governors Association/National Association of State Units on Aging, 1988.

Dislocated Workers: Local Programs and Outcomes Under the Job Training Partnership Act. Washington, D.C.: U.S. General Accounting Office, 1987.

Knuti, D., and Zuckerman, A. (eds.). *JTPA Programs and Activities.* Berkeley, Calif.: Center for Community Futures, 1986.

Making JTPA Work for Older Persons: A National Catalogue of Practical How-To's. Washington, D.C.: National Association of State Units on Aging, 1987.

Memory Enhancement

Garfunkel, F., and Landau, G. *A Memory Retention Course for the Aged.* Washington, D.C.: National Council on the Aging, 1981.

Light, L., and Burke, D. M. (eds.). *Language, Memory, and Aging.* New York: Cambridge University Press, 1988.
Meyer, B. J. *Memory Improved: Increased Reading Comprehension and Memory for Young and Old Adults.* Hillsdale, N.J.: Erlbaum, 1988.
Stern, L. *Improving Your Memory: A Guide for Older Adults.* Ann Arbor, Mich.: Turner Geriatric Services, University of Michigan Medical Center, 1987.

Multicultural Work Force

Also see publications list of the Society for Intercultural Education, Training and Research (SIETAR), 1505 22nd St. NW, Washington, D.C. 20037.

Arndt, M. "Cross-Cultural Corporate Awakening." *Chicago Tribune,* May 28, 1989, sec. 7.
Copeland, L. "Cross-Cultural Training: The Competitive Edge." *Training,* 1985, *22,* 49–53.
Copeland, L. "Learning to Manage a Multicultural Workforce." *Training,* 1988, 25, 48–58.
Dodd, C. H. *Dynamics of Intercultural Communication.* Dubuque, Iowa: Brown, 1987.
Harris, P. R., and Moran, R. T. *Managing Cultural Differences.* Houston, Tex.: Gulf Publishing Company, 1987.
Plummer, J. "Changing Values." *The Futurist,* 1989, *23*(1), 8–13.
Sowell, T. *Ethnic America.* New York: Basic Books, 1981.

Organizational Norms Concerning Age

Lawrence, B. S. "Age Grading: The Implicit Organizational Timetable." *Journal of Occupational Behavior,* 1984, *5,* 23–35.
Lawrence, B. S. "An Organizational Theory of Age Effects." In S. Bacharach and N. D. Tomaso (eds.). *Research in the Sociology of Organizations.* Vol. 5. Greenwich, Conn.: JAI Press, 1987.
Lawrence, B. S. "New Wrinkles in the Theory of Age: Demography, Norms, and Performance Ratings." *Academy of Management Journal,* 1988, *31*(2), 309–337.

Retirement Planning and Programs

See also the "Alternative Work Options" category, above. These works often describe corporate retirement programs.

Dennis, H. *Retirement Preparation: What Retirement Specialists Need to Know.* Lexington, Mass.: Lexington Books, 1984.

McFadden, J. J. *Retirement Plans for Employees.* Homewood, Ill.: Irwin, 1988.

Morrison, M. H., and Jedrziewski, M. K. "Retirement Planning: Everybody Benefits." *Personnel Administrator,* 1988, *33,* 74–80.

Siebert, E. H., and Siebert, J. S. (eds.). *Resource Guide for Preretirement Planning.* (Rev. ed.) Janesville, Wis.: Siebert Associates, 1989.

Stereotypes About Age

See also the "General Interest" category, above. Most of these works discuss myths and stereotypes of aging.

Nye, D. "Writing Off Assets." *Across the Board,* 1988, *25,* 44–52.

Rosen, B., and Jerdee, T. H. "The Influence of Age Stereotypes on Managerial Decisions." *Journal of Applied Psychology,* 1976a, *61,* 428–432.

Rosen, B., and Jerdee, T. H. "The Nature of Job-Related Age Stereotypes." *Journal of Applied Psychology,* 1976b, *62,* 180–183.

Rosen, B., and Jerdee, T. H. "Too Old or Not Too Old." *Harvard Business Review,* 1977, *55,* 97–107.

Wellness and Older Workers

"Businesses Develop Wellness Programs for Older Employees." *Working Age,* 1987, *3*(2), 3.

Dychtwald, K. *Wellness and Health Promotion for the Elderly.* Rockville, Md.: Aspen Systems, 1986.

Levin, R. *Wellness for Older Workers and Retirees.* Washington, D.C.: Washington Business Group on Health, 1987.

U.S. Department of Health and Human Services. *National Survey of Worksite Health Promotion Activities.* (Unpublished manuscript.) Washington, D.C.: Office of Disease Prevention and Health Promotion, 1986.

Women and Aging

Health and Economic Status of Women. Farmingdale, N.Y.: Baywood, 1989.

Herz, D. E. "Employment Characteristics of Older Women, 1987." *Monthly Labor Review,* 1988, *111*(9), 3-12.

Older Women's League. *Report on the Status of Midlife and Older Women in America.* Washington, D.C.: Older Women's League, 1986.

Seskin, J. *More Than Mere Survival: Conversations with Women over 65.* New York: Newsweek Books, 1980.

U.S. Congress. House. Select Committee on Aging. *The Quality of Life for Older Women Living Alone.* 100th Cong., 2d sess., Dec. 1988. Washington, D.C.: U.S. Government Printing Office, 1988.

Women in the Later Years: Health, Social, and Cultural Perspectives. Women and Health Series, *14*(3-4). Binghamton, N.Y.: Haworth Press, 1988.

"Women in the Workplace." *Working Age,* 1988, *3(4), 1-8.*

References

"The Aging Workforce." *The Aging Workforce,* 1987, *1*(1), 1–8.

American Association of Retired Persons. *Older Employees Offer . . . Results of Yankelovich, Skelly, White Survey.* Washington, D.C.: American Association of Retired Persons, 1985a.

American Association of Retired Persons. *Workers over 50: Old Myths, New Realities.* Washington, D.C.: American Association of Retired Persons, 1985b.

American Association of Retired Persons. *Managing a Changing Work Force.* Washington, D.C.: American Association of Retired Persons, 1986a.

American Association of Retired Persons. *Older Workers: Information Sheet.* Washington, D.C.: American Association of Retired Persons, 1986b.

American Association of Retired Persons. *Truth About Aging.* Washington, D.C.: American Association of Retired Persons, 1986c.

American Association of Retired Persons. *Work and Retirement: Employees over 40 and Their Views.* Washington, D.C.: American Association of Retired Persons, 1986d.

American Association of Retired Persons. *Workers 45 + : Today and Tomorrow.* Washington, D.C.: American Association of Retired Persons, 1986e.

American Association of Retired Persons. *A Profile of Older Americans.* Washington, D.C.: American Association of Retired Persons, 1987.

American Association of Retired Persons. *Aging in America: Dignity or Despair?* Washington, D.C.: American Association of Retired Persons, 1988a.

American Association of Retired Persons. *Using the Experience of a Lifetime.* Washington, D.C.: American Association of Retired Persons, 1988b.

Ansley, J., and Erber, J. T. "Computer Interaction: Effect on Attitudes and Performance in Older Adults." *Educational Gerontology,* 1988, *14*(2), 107–121.

Axel, H. *Job Banks for Retirees.* New York: The Conference Board, 1989.

Bardwick, J. M. *The Plateauing Trap.* New York: AMACOM, 1986.

Belbin, R. M. "The Discovery Method in Training Older Workers." In H. L. Sheppard (ed.), *Toward an Industrial Gerontology.* Cambridge, Mass.: Schenkman, 1970.

Bird, C. "The Jobs You Dream About." *Modern Maturity,* 1988, *31*(1), 30–37.

Blake, R. R., and Mouton, J. S. "The Management Grid III." *Personnel Psychology,* 1986, *39,* 238–240.

Bolles, R. N. *The 1988 What Color Is Your Parachute?* Berkeley, Calif.: Ten Speed Press, 1988.

Bracker, J. S., and Pearson, J. N. "Worker Obsolescence: The Human Resource Dilemma of the '80s." *Personnel Administrator,* 1986, *31,* 109–116.

Bridges, W. "The Discovery of Middle Age." *Human Behavior,* 1977, *6,* 65–68.

Bureau of National Affairs. *Older Americans in the Workforce: Challenges and Solutions.* Washington, D.C.: Bureau of National Affairs, 1987.

Burns, G. *How to Live to Be a Hundred.* New York: Putnam, 1983.

"Businesses Develop Wellness Programs for Older Employees." *Working Age,* 1987, *3*(2), 3.

Butler, R. *Aging and Mental Health.* St. Louis, Mo.: Mosby, 1973.

"CAD/CAM and the Older Worker." *Working Age,* 1988, *4*(1), 6–7.

Casner-Lotto, J. "Hewlett-Packard: Partnerships for New Careers." In J. Casner-Lotto and Associates, *Successful Training*

Strategies: Twenty-Six Innovations Corporate Models. San Francisco: Jossey-Bass, 1988.

Christensen, K. *Flexible Staffing and Scheduling in U.S. Corporations.* New York: The Conference Board, 1989.

Clark, M. "An Anthropological View of Retirement." In F. Carp (ed.), *Retirement.* New York: Behavioral Publications, 1972.

Coberly, S. "Keeping Older Workers on the Job." *Aging,* 1985, *349,* 23–26.

The Colonel's Tradition Brochure. Louisville, Ky.: Kentucky Fried Chicken, 1988.

"Companies Gear Up Programs to Train Older Workers." *Older American Reports,* 1988, *10*(38), 1–2.

"Conference Explores an Older Work Force." *Restaurant Business,* Sept. 1, 1987, pp. 48–49.

Connelly, K. "Older Workers Find Place in the Lodging Industry." *Hotel and Motel Management,* Sept. 28, 1987, pp. 22, 68–69.

Control Data. NOWIS Information Summary no. 1069. Washington, D.C.: American Association of Retired Persons, 1987.

"Corporate Ideas for Effective Work Force Management." *Working Age,* 1988, *3*(5), 2.

Cox, H. *Later Life.* Englewood Cliffs, N.J.: Prentice-Hall, 1984.

Crouse-Hinds ECM. NOWIS Information Summary no. 1005. Washington, D.C.: American Association of Retired Persons, 1987.

Dangott, L., and Kalish, R. *A Time to Enjoy the Pleasures of Aging.* Englewood Cliffs, N.J.: Prentice-Hall, 1979.

Davis, I. A., and Taguri, R. "Using Life-Stage Theory to Manage Work Relationships." In H. Dennis (ed.), *Fourteen Steps in Managing an Aging Work Force.* Lexington, Mass.: Heath, 1988.

"Days Inns, NCOA Collaborate on Giant Job Fair." *The Aging Workforce,* 1988, *2*(4), 8.

Dennis, H. *Fourteen Steps in Managing an Aging Work Force.* Lexington, Mass.: Heath, 1988.

Dennis, H., and Peterson, D. A. "Training Managers of Older Workers: Implications for Industrial Gerontology." *Gerontology and Geriatrics Education,* 1983, *4*(1), 53–60.

Doering, M., Rhodes, S., and Schuster, M. *The Aging Worker: Research and Recommendations.* Newbury Park, Calif.: Sage, 1983.

Dychtwald, K. *Wellness and Health Promotion for the Elderly.* Rockville, Md.: Aspen, 1986.

Dychtwald, K. *Age Wave: The Challenges and Opportunities of an Aging America.* Los Angeles: Tarcher, 1989.

"Eldercare a Key Employee Benefit at Champion International." *The Aging Workforce,* 1987, *1*(1), 7.

"Eldercare Is an Emerging Employee Benefit." *The Aging Workforce,* 1988, *2*(2), 3.

"Eldercare: The Emerging Employee Benefit." *Working Age,* 1990, *5*(4), 3, 5.

The Elder Craftsman. NOWIS Information Summary no. 1122. Washington, D.C.: American Association of Retired Persons, 1987.

"Employers' Greatest Concern: Recruiting and Retaining Good Employees." *Working Age,* 1989, *5*(2), 5, 91–98.

Fitzgerald, T. H. "The Loss of Work: Notes from Retirement." *Harvard Business Review,* 1988, *66*(2), 99–103.

Fraze, J. "Displaced Workers: Oakies of the '80s." *Personnel Administrator,* 1988, *33*(1), 42–51.

Garfunkel, F., and Landau, G. *A Memory Retention Course for the Aged.* Washington, D.C.: National Council on the Aging, 1981.

Gist, M., Rosen, B., and Schwoerer, C. "The Influence of Training Method and Trainee Age on the Acquisition of Computer Skills." *Personnel Psychology,* 1988, *41,* 255–265.

Glasse, L. "The Economic Insecurity of Older Women." In Metropolitan Chicago Coalition on Aging (ed.), *The Business of Growing Older: Is It a Women Issue?* Chicago: Metropolitan Chicago Coalition on Aging, 1988.

Goddard, R. W. "How to Harness America's Gray Power." *Personnel Journal,* 1987, *66,* 33–34.

Gutteridge, T. G., and Hutcheson, P. G. "Career Development." In L. Nadler (ed.), *The Handbook of Human Resource Development.* New York: Wiley, 1984.

Hall, V. M., and Wessel, J. A. "Attention Is Focused on Problem Status of Older Workers." *Atlanta Constitution,* Mar. 9, 1986, p. 1.

Harvey, R. L., and Jahns, I. R. "Using Advance Organizers to Facilitate Learning Among Older Adults." *Educational Gerontology*, 1988, *14*(2), 89–93.

Havighurst, R. J. *Developmental Tasks and Education*. New York: McKay, 1973.

Heisler, W. J., Jones, W. D., and Benham, P. O. *Managing Human Resources Issues: Confronting Challenges and Choosing Options*. San Francisco: Jossey-Bass, 1988.

Hersey, P., and Blanchard, K. *Management of Organizational Behavior*. (5th ed.) Englewood Cliffs, N.J.: Prentice-Hall, 1988.

Herz, D. E. "Employment Characteristics of Older Women, 1987." *Monthly Labor Review*, 1988, *111*(9), 3–12.

Hickey, J. V. "A Participative Approach to a Technological Challenge: General Electric Company's Aerospace Electronic Systems Department." In J. Casner-Lotto and Associates (eds.), *Successful Training Strategies: Twenty-Six Innovative Corporate Models*. San Francisco: Jossey-Bass, 1988a.

Hickey, J. V. "The Travelers Corporation: Expanding Computer Literacy in the Organization." In J. Casner-Lotto and Associates (eds.), *Successful Training Strategies: Twenty-Six Innovative Corporate Models*. San Francisco: Jossey-Bass, 1988b.

"Hiring Older Americans: A National Strategy." *Progress Index* (Petersburg, Va.), Aug. 4, 1987, p. 1.

House, R. J., and Mitchell, T. R. "Path-Goal Theory of Leadership." *Journal of Contemporary Business*, 1974, 81–98.

Humple, C., and Lyons, M. *Management and the Older Workforce*. New York: American Management Association, 1983.

"IBM Promotes Flexibility to Attract and Retain Skilled Workers." *The Aging Workforce*, 1988, *2*(4), 2.

"Improve Your Bottom Line. Hire Older Workers Say Business Leaders at National Conference." *The Aging Workforce*, 1989, *3*(1), 1–3.

International Executive Service Corps. NOWIS Information Summary no. 1132. Washington, D.C.: American Association of Retired Persons, 1987.

Jacobson, B. *Young Programs for Older Workers*. New York: Van Nostrand Reinhold, 1980.

John, M. T. *Geragogy: A Theory for Teaching the Elderly.* New York: Haworth Press, 1988.

Johnston, W. B., and Packer, A. H. *Workforce 2000: Work and Workers for the Twenty-first Century.* Indianapolis, Ind.: Hudson Institute, 1987.

Kahne, H. "Not Yet Equal: Employment Experience of Older Women and Older Men." *International Journal of Aging and Human Development,* 1985, *22*(1), 1–13.

Kaminski–da–Roza, V. "A Workshop That Optimizes the Older Worker's Productivity." *Personnel,* 1984, *61, 47*–56.

Karp, D. A. "A Decade of Reminders: Changing Age Consciousness Between Fifty and Sixty Years Old." *The Gerontologist,* 1988, *28*(6), 727–738.

Kelly Services, Inc. NOWIS Information Summary no. 1203. Washington, D.C.: American Association of Retired Persons, 1987.

KFC Works for Older Workers. Louisville, Ky.: Kentucky Fried Chicken, n.d.

Kottman, W. "Is 'Contingent' Work Good for Older Workers— and for Businesses?" *The Aging Workforce,* 1988, *2*(3), 4.

Kravetz, D. *The Human Resources Revolution: Implementing Progressive Management Practices for Bottom-Line Success.* San Francisco: Jossey-Bass, 1988.

Kuchta, W. "How to Let Demographics Work for *Your* Company." *The Aging Workforce,* 1988, *2*(3), 2.

Lantos, T. *Opening Statement,* May 19, 1988. U.S. Congress. Senate. Subcommittee on Employment and Housing. Washington, D.C.: U.S. Government Printing Office, 1988.

Lawrence, B. S. "New Wrinkles in the Theory of Age: Demography, Norms and Performance Ratings." *Academy of Management Journal,* 1988, *31,* 309–337.

Lazarus, J., and Lauer, H. "Working Past Retirement: Practical and Motivational Issues." In R. N. Butler (ed.), *Productive Aging.* New York: Springer, 1985.

Lee, J. A., and Clemons, T. "Factors Affecting Employment Decisions About Older Workers." *Journal of Applied Psychology,* 1985, *70*(4), 785–788.

Lester, B. *A Practitioner's Guide for Training Older Workers.* Washington, D.C.: National Commission for Employment Policy, 1985.

Levin, R. C. *Wellness Programs for Older Workers and Retirees.* Washington, D.C.: Business Group on Health, 1987.

Lieberman, L., and Lieberman, L. "The Second Career Concept." *Aging and Work,* 1983, *6*(4), 277–290.

McDonnell, S. R. "Assessing the Health and Job Performance of Older Workers." *Business and Health,* 1984, *20,* 18–22.

"McDonald's, with an Assist from NCOA, to Offer Management Openings to Older Workers." *Perspective on Aging,* 1988, *17*(6), 8.

McMasters Brochure. Oak Brook, Ill.: McDonald's, 1988.

"Major Survey Report: Companies Should Do More for Careers of Older Workers." *The Aging Workforce,* 1988, *2*(3), 103.

Maryland New Directions. NOWIS Information Summary no. 1172. Washington, D.C.: American Association of Retired Persons, 1987.

Match, S. K. "A New Look at Companies That Hire Experience." *Perspective on Aging,* 1987, *16,* 18–22.

Meier, E. L. *Employment Experience and Income of Older Women.* Washington, D.C.: American Association of Retired Persons, 1986.

Memmott, M. "Old Hands Return, Find Fulfillment." *USA Today,* Aug. 4, 1986, pp. 1–2.

Mercer, W. M., Inc. *Employer Attitudes: Implications of an Aging Workforce.* New York: William M. Mercer, Inc. [marketing research firm], 1981.

Mintz, F. "Retraining: The Graying of the Training Room." *Personnel,* 1986, *63,* 69–71.

Mizock, M. "Senior Citizens—DP's Untapped Reservoir." *Data Management,* 1986, *24,* 20.

Mullan, C., and Gorman, L. "Facilitating Adaptation to Change: A Case Study in Retraining Middle-Aged and Older Workers at *Aer Lingus.*" *Industrial Gerontology,* 1972, *15,* 20–39.

The Myths and Realities of Aging. Pima, Ariz.: Long-Term Care Administration Program, University of Arizona, 1979.

Nadler, N. "Human Resource Development." In L. Nadler (ed.), *The Handbook of Human Resource Development.* New York: Wiley, 1984.

Nadler, L., and Nadler, Z. *Developing Human Resources: Concepts and a Model.* (3rd ed.) San Francisco: Jossey-Bass, 1989.

National Alliance of Business. *Invest in Experience: New Directions for an Aging Workforce.* Washington, D.C.: National Alliance of Business, 1985.

National Commission for Employment Policy. *Older-Worker Employment Comes of Age: Practice and Potential.* Washington, D.C.: National Commission for Employment Policy, 1985.

National Commission on Working Women. *Women, Work and Age: A Report on Older Women and Employment.* Washington, D.C.: National Commission on Working Women, 1987.

National Council on the Aging National Work Group. "The Older Worker as a Lifelong Achiever Training Module." Training module presented at National Council on the Aging annual conference, Washington, D.C., Apr. 1988.

Neugarten, B. L. "Adaptation and the Life Cycle." *Counseling Psychologist,* 1976, *6,* 16–20.

New Career Opportunities, Inc. NOWIS Information Summary no. 1. Washington, D.C.: American Association of Retired Persons, 1987.

"New Strategies Can Motivate Plateaued, Other Older Workers." *Ideas and Trends in Personnel,* July 26, 1989, pp. 134–135.

Odiorne, D. "Managing GRAMPIES." *Training,* 1988, *25*(6), 37–39.

Oldenburg, D. "Loyalty and the Workplace." *Washington Post,* Jan. 5, 1988, p. B5.

Older Women's League. *Report on the Status of Midlife and Older Women in America.* Washington, D.C.: Older Women's League, 1986.

"Older Workers." *Trends and Issues Alert* [fact sheet]. Columbus, Ohio: National Center for Research in Vocational Education, 1988.

Paul, C. E. *A Human Resource Management Perspective on Work Alternatives for Older Workers.* Research Report Series. Washington, D.C.: National Commission for Economic Policy, 1983.

Paul, C. E. "Work Alternatives for Older Americans." In S. H. Sandell (ed.), *The Problem Isn't Age.* New York: Praeger, 1987.

Paul, C. E. "Implementing Alternative Work Arrangements for Older Workers." In H. Dennis (ed.), *Fourteen Steps to Managing an Aging Workforce.* Lexington, Mass.: Heath, 1988.

Perlmutter, M. "Cognitive Potential Throughout Life." In J. Birren (ed.), *Emergent Theories of Aging.* New York: Springer, 1988.

Peterson, D. A. *Facilitating Education for Older Learners.* San Francisco: Jossey-Bass, 1983.

Peterson, J., and Rosenblatt, R. "Care of Aged Takes Toll on Families." *Los Angeles Times,* Apr. 6, 1986, pp. 2, 10.

Piktialis, D. "Caregiving: Employers' Perspectives and Business Practices." In Metropolitan Chicago Coalition on Aging (ed.), *The Business of Growing Older: Is It a Women's Issue?* Chicago: Metropolitan Chicago Coalition on Aging, 1988.

Pitney Bowes, Inc. NOWIS Information Summary no. 1033. Washington, D.C.: American Association of Retired Persons, 1987.

"Press Release: The Colonel's Tradition." Louisville, Ky.: Kentucky Fried Chicken, 1988.

"Productivity Increases As Employees Age." *Working Age,* 1986, *2*(3), 5.

"Promoting Older Women's Employment Rights." *Working Age,* 1988, *4*(3), 5.

"Research Findings: Older Persons Can Excel on Computers." *The Aging Workforce,* 1989, *3*(1), 5.

Retirement Advisors. "Open Forum." *Insights,* Winter 1988, pp. 1-2.

Robinson, P. K. *Organizational Strategies for Older Workers.* Work in America Studies in Productivity. New York: Pergamon Press, 1983.

Root, L. S. "Corporate Programs for Older Workers." *Aging,* 1985, *351,* 12-16.

Root, L. S., and Zarrugh, L. H. "Private Sector Employment Practices for Older Workers." In S. H. Sandell (ed.), *The Problem Isn't Age.* New York: Praeger, 1987.

Rosen, B. "Management Perceptions of Older Employees." *Monthly Labor Review: Conference Papers.* Washington, D.C.: Bureau of Labor Statistics, May 1978.

Rosen, B., and Jerdee, J. H. "Helping Young Managers Bridge the Generation Gap." *Training,* 1985a, *22*(3), 42-51.

Rosen, B., and Jerdee, J. H. "A Model Program for Combating Employee Obsolescence." *Personnel Administrator,* 1985b, *30*(3), 86-92.

Rosen, B., and Jerdee, J. H. *Older Employees: New Roles for Valued Resources.* Homewood, Ill.: Dow Jones-Irwin, 1985c.

Rosen, B., and Jerdee, J. H. "Investing in the Older Worker." *Personnel Administrator,* 1989, *34*(4), 70–74.

Roundtable on Older Women in the Workforce. *Roundtable on Older Women in the Workforce: Proceedings and Recommendations.* Washington, D.C.: American Association of Retired Persons, 1988.

Rubenstein, R. "Aerospace: Options to Encourage Work After 65." *Generations,* 1982, *6,* 61–62.

Rupp, K., Bryant, E., Mantovani, R., and Rhoads, M. "Government Employment and Training Programs, and Older Americans." In S. H. Sandell (ed.), *The Problem Isn't Age.* New York: Praeger, 1987.

Sandell, S. H. (ed.). *The Problem Isn't Age: Work and Older Americans.* New York: Praeger, 1987.

Sandell, S. H. "Public Policies and Programs Affecting Older Workers." In M. Berkowitz and Associates (eds.), *The Older Worker.* Madison, Wis.: Industrial Relations Research Association, 1988.

Santrock, J. W. *Adult Development and Aging.* Dubuque, Iowa: Brown, 1985.

Schein, E. H. "The Individual, the Organization, and the Career: A Conceptual Scheme." *Journal of Applied Behavioral Science,* 1971, *7*(4), 415–416.

Schein, E. H. *Career Dynamics.* Reading, Mass.: Addison-Wesley, 1978.

Schein, E. H. *Career Anchors: Discovering Your Real Values.* San Diego, Calif.: University Associates, 1985.

Schulz, R. *Adult Development and Aging.* New York: Macmillan, 1988.

Seltzer, M. "Myths and Stereotypes About Older Women." In U.S. Senate, Special Committee on Aging (ed.), *Women in Our Aging Society.* Washington, D.C.: U.S. Government Printing Office, 1984.

Simonsen, P. "Concepts of Career Development." *Training and Development Journal,* 1986, *40,* 70–74.

Singleton, W. T. "Age, Skill, and Management." *International Journal of Aging and Human Development,* 1983, *17*(1), 15–23.

Sonnenfeld, J. "Dealing with the Aging Work Force." *Harvard Business Review,* 1978, *56*(6), 81–92.

Stein, S. "Creative Strategies Make Older Workers Welcome at McDonald's." *The Aging Workforce,* 1988, *2*(4), 1, 3.

Sterns, H., and Doverspike, D. "Training and Developing the Older Worker." In H. Dennis (ed.), *Fourteen Steps to Managing an Aging Workforce.* Lexington, Mass.: Heath, 1988.

Stouffer Foods Corporation. NOWIS Information Summary no. 1023. Washington, D.C.: American Association of Retired Persons, 1987.

Tannenbaum, R., and Schmidt, W. H. "How to Choose a Leadership Pattern." *Harvard Business Review,* 1958, *37*(2), 95–102.

Taylor, S. "The Aging of America." *Training and Development Journal,* 1989, *43*(10), 44–52.

Texas Refinery Corporation. NOWIS Information Summary no. 1040. Washington, D.C.: American Association of Retired Persons, 1987.

Toufexis, A. "Grays on the Go." *Time,* Fed. 22, 1988, pp. 66–79.

"Understanding Older Workers." *Working Age,* 1985, *1*(3), 4.

U.S. Department of Health and Human Services, Administration on Aging. Office of Human Development Services. *Older Workers: Myths and Reality.* Washington, D.C.: U.S. Department of Health and Human Services, Administration on Aging, 1986.

U.S. Senate, Special Committee on Aging. *Personnel Practices for an Aging Workforce: Private Sector Examples.* 99th Cong., 1st sess. Washington, D.C.: U.S. Government Printing Office, 1985.

Vaillant, G. *Adaptation to Life.* Boston: Little, Brown, 1977.

"Wal-Mart." *The Aging Workforce,* 1988, *2*(4), 7.

Webster's New Collegiate Dictionary. (9th ed.) Springfield, Mass.: Merriam, 1977.

Winfield, F. E. "Workplace Solutions for Women Under Eldercare Pressure." *Personnel Journal,* 1987, *64*(7), 31–39.

Wisconsin Bureau on Aging. *Older-Worker Training.* Technical Assistance Pamphlet no. 2. Madison: Wisconsin Bureau on Aging, n.d.

"Women in the Workplace." *Working Age,* 1988, *3*(4), 1–8.

Women's Bureau, U.S. Department of Labor. *Earnings Difference Between Women and Men Workers.* Fact sheet no. 85-7. Washington, D.C.: Women's Bureau, U.S. Department of Labor, 1985.

Women's Bureau, U.S. Department of Labor. *Women Who Maintain Families.* Fact sheet no. 86-2. Washington, D.C.: Women's Bureau, U.S. Department of Labor, 1986a.

Women's Bureau, U.S. Department of Labor. *Caring for Elderly Family Members.* Fact sheet no. 86-4. Washington, D.C.: Women's Bureau, U.S. Department of Labor, 1986b.

Worker Equity Department, American Association of Retired Persons. *How to Manage Older Workers.* Washington, D.C.: American Association of Retired Persons, 1988a.

Worker Equity Department, American Association of Retired Persons. *How to Train Older Workers.* Washington, D.C.: American Association of Retired Persons, 1988b.

Workforce 2000, Executive Summary: The Nation's Workforce, Year 2000. National Conference on the Nation's Workforce, Year 2000. Oct. 24–26, 1988.

Yankelovich, D., and Associates. *Aging in America: Current Trends and Future Directions.* New York: Markle Foundation, 1988.

Index

Index